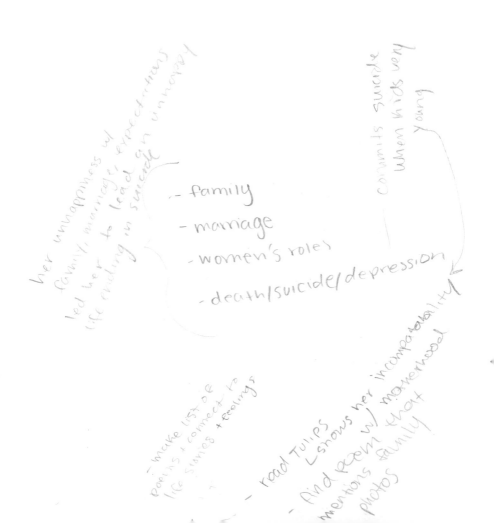

her unhappiness w/
Covey, marriage, expectations
led her to lead an unhappy
life ending in suicide

- family
- marriage
- women's roles
- death/suicide/depression

commits suicide
when kids very
young

- make list of
poems + connect to
life stories + feelings

- read Tulips
 └ shows her incompatability
   w/ motherhood
- find poem that
mentions family
photos

# Sylvia Plath, Revised

## Twayne's United States Authors Series

Joseph M. Flora, Editor

*University of North Carolina, Chapel Hill*

TUSAS 702

SYLVIA PLATH
*AP/Wide World Photos*

# *Sylvia Plath, Revised*

## Caroline King Barnard Hall

*Pennsylvania State University*

Twayne Publishers

New York

Twayne's United States Author Series No. 702

*Sylvia Plath, Revised*
Caroline King Barnard Hall

Twayne Publishers

1633 Broadway
New York, NY 10019

**Library of Congress Cataloging-in-Publication Data**

Hall, Caroline King Barnard.
    Sylvia Plath, Revised / Caroline King Barnard Hall.
        p. cm. — (Twayne's United States authors series ; TUSAS 702)
    Includes bibliographical references (p.     ) and index.
    ISBN 0-8057-7838-1 (acid-free paper)
        1. Plath, Sylvia—Criticism and interpretation. 2. Women and literature—United States—History—20th century.    I. Title.
    II. Series.
PS3566.L27Z675  1998
811'.54—dc21                                                      98-10002
                                                                        CIP

This paper meets the requirements of ANSI/NISO Z3948-1992 (Permanence of Paper).

10 9 8 7 6 5 4 3 2

Printed in the United States of America

*For Tim*

# Contents

# Preface

Much has happened in Plath studies during the 20 years since I wrote the first edition of *Sylvia Plath* (1978). Interest in Plath's work has continued to increase steadily; Plath's autobiographical novel, *The Bell Jar,* has by now become standard fare in high school curricula and in university literature courses, and *Ariel* has remained a vital subject of study for students and scholars alike. Of great importance for Plath's readers are the primary works that have been published, most notably *Johnny Panic and the Bible of Dreams* (1977 and 1979), a collection of short stories and prose edited by Ted Hughes; *The Collected Poems* (1981), a chronologically arranged volume that includes some previously uncollected poems, also edited by Hughes; and *The Journals of Sylvia Plath* (1982), a selection of Plath's 1950–1962 journals, edited by Hughes and Frances McCullough. During the past decade, major secondary material has also appeared; of particular note are the biographies and critical-biographical studies that have contributed new information and spirited controversy to Plath scholarship.

These new developments have captured the attention of student readers and scholars alike, particularly with regard to the complex and enigmatic relationship between Plath's poetry and personality in the few years preceding her suicide. The publication of four major biographies and two critical-biographical studies in the seven years between 1987 and 1994 has sparked lively interest in the interpretation of Plath's life events and in the effect of those events upon the poet's creative output. The appearance of *The Collected Poems* has generated especially spirited discussion about the poems' chronology, the contents of *Ariel,* and the editors' decision making. As more plentiful material has become available, readers have engaged in debate not only about that material itself but also about the manner of its appearance. In their practice of publishing poetry, journals, and manuscripts piecemeal, Plath's literary executors and editors have simultaneously gratified readers and raised questions about selection and control.

Part of my purpose in revising my 1978 *Sylvia Plath* is to take notice of these intriguing and substantial developments while stressing my earlier emphasis on the continuity of Plath's posthumous reputation as a fine poet and a good fiction writer. Whereas a chronological study of

Plath's work continues to lead to a fuller understanding of her best, late poems, there is now much more to review and understand. Even the very character of *Ariel,* her finest volume, has been altered by Hughes's revelations about his tinkering with the poems' selection and order. In this edition, therefore, I have provided new chapters to examine the biographies and the *Journals,* expanded the *Bell Jar* chapter to include analysis of *Johnny Panic,* rewritten and refocused the concluding chapter to evaluate directions in Plath scholarship, and augmented the other chapters to reflect new developments in both primary and secondary sources. There is much to discuss, and I hope that readers will find in this new edition a reliable and interesting overview of the recent and present state of Plath studies.

# Acknowledgments

My quotations are taken from the American editions of *The Bell Jar, The Colossus, Crossing the Water, Winter Trees, Ariel, Johnny Panic and the Bible of Dreams,* and *The Collected Poems.* Each of these books (with the exception of *The Collected Poems*) was first published in England; in the case of the individual poetry volumes and *Johnny Panic,* the contents of the British and American versions differ slightly. I have described these differences at the beginning of the relevant chapters or sections.

For their advice, counsel, and support in various indispensable ways, I wish to thank the friends, professors, colleagues, and family members whom I acknowledged in the preface to my 1978 *Sylvia Plath:* Warren French, Robert Scholes, Keith Waldrop, Mark Spilka, Daniel Marder, Richard Harlow, York King, Margaret King, and J. B. Wolgamot. Because this revised edition grows from my original book, I remain grateful to these individuals, to the Brown University libraries, and to the University of New Orleans Organized Research Fund.

I also wish to acknowledge those who have helped me in preparing this revised edition. For their efficiency and cheerfulness in assisting me with my research, I thank the librarians at the Beaver Campus of Penn State, particularly Martin Goldberg, head librarian. For their sensitive and invaluable editorial suggestions, I am indebted to Joseph M. Flora, general editor of Twayne's United States Authors Series, and to Impressions Book and Journal Services. For her guidance in the preparation of my manuscript, I am grateful to Anne Davidson, editor at Twayne. For being a great cook on the many evenings when I worked late, I thank my husband, John Reynolds Hall.

By dedicating my book to my brother Timothy Alfred King, I mean also to acknowledge the enduring support of my family: my parents, Margaret and York King; my brother Dave, and Elizabeth and Chris; my husband, John; his mother, Jacelyn Hall, and his recently deceased father, Broyles Hall; and the rest of our extended family. In the years I have worked on the two versions of this book, we have together experienced momentous changes. My new marriage inspired the dedication of my original *Sylvia Plath* to my husband; the recent death of my beloved brother Tim occasions the dedication of this revision, which is at once an ending and a beginning.

# Chronology

1932    October 27, Sylvia Plath born in Boston, the first child of Aurelia Schober and Otto Emil Plath.

1936    Family (including younger brother, Warren, born 1935) moves to seaside town of Winthrop, Massachusetts.

1940    Father dies.

1942    Family moves inland to Wellesley, Massachusetts.

1942–1950    Attends public schools in Wellesley. Writes first poems and short stories.

1950    Receives scholarship to Smith College.

1953    Spends summer in New York as *Mademoiselle* guest editor. Returns home to Wellesley; attempts suicide; is hospitalized.

1954    Returns to Smith; receives scholarship to Harvard summer school.

1955    Graduates from Smith; attends Cambridge University, England, on Fulbright fellowship.

1956    June 16, marries Ted Hughes.

1957    Returns with husband to Massachusetts; teaches English for one year at Smith College.

1958    Resides in Boston; writes and attends Robert Lowell's poetry classes at Boston University.

1959    Visits Yaddo Colony; returns to England; resides in London.

1960    April 1, Frieda Rebecca Hughes born. October, publishes *The Colossus and Other Poems* in Great Britain.

1961    Family moves to Devon.

1962    January 17, Nicholas Farrar Hughes born. May, publishes *The Colossus and Other Poems* in the United States. December, separated from husband, moves with children to London.

1963    January, publishes *The Bell Jar* under the pseudonym Victoria Lucas. February 11, commits suicide.

1965    *Ariel* published in Great Britain.

1966    *Ariel* published in the United States.

1967    *The Bell Jar* published in Great Britain under Plath's own name.

1971    *The Bell Jar* and *Crossing the Water* published in the United States. *Crossing the Water* and *Winter Trees* published in Great Britain.

1972    *Winter Trees* published in the United States.

1975    *Letters Home* published in the United States.

1976    *Letters Home* published in Great Britain.

        *The Bed Book* published.

1977    *Johnny Panic and the Bible of Dreams* published in Great Britain.

1979    *Johnny Panic and the Bible of Dreams* published in the United States.

1981    *Collected Poems* published in the United States and Great Britain.

1982    *The Journals of Sylvia Plath* published in the United States.

## Chapter One

# The Life That Shaped the Work

Sylvia Plath is a writer whose life has generated unusually keen interest. Such interest is provoked, no doubt, partly by her tragic and untimely death and partly by the highly personal nature of her writings. She strikes a responsive chord in her readers; many can see in Esther Greenwood, the autobiographical narrator of Plath's very popular novel, *The Bell Jar*, something of themselves. And the intense emotional content of her poems, especially of those included in *Ariel*, evoke awe even in those readers who only partially understand them. Examining Plath's life does, indeed, illuminate one's understanding of her work, for much of the imagery, attitudes, and events in Plath's poetry and fiction have their genesis in her life experience. A major biographical objective, then, should be the discovery of the self that is constantly being re-created in the literature. For Sylvia Plath, biography is significant ultimately because of her perception of it.

## Seaside Childhood

Throughout her short life, Sylvia Plath loved and was fascinated by the sea. She spent her early years close by the ocean on the Atlantic coast just north of Boston, and this childhood place was marvelous to her, not only inspiring wonder and awe but also providing the source for much of her later poetic imagery. Indeed, as she writes in one of her letters home, "my ocean-childhood . . . is probably the foundation of my consciousness."[1]

Sylvia Plath was born in Boston, Massachusetts, on October 27, 1932, to Aurelia Schober Plath and Otto Emil Plath. Her father, a professor of biology and German at Boston University, was of German descent, having emigrated from Grabow, in the Polish Corridor, when he was 15. Her mother was a first-generation American, born in Boston of Austrian parents. Their common Germanic background was indirectly responsible for their meeting; they met in 1929 when Aurelia Schober, working on a master's degree in English and German at Boston University, took a German course taught by Otto Plath. Their common

1

Germanic background was also to become very important to the poetic life of their daughter, Sylvia, for it, like the sea, provided a major source for her poetic imagery.

Otto Plath seems to have been guided by the principles of discipline and order; as Aurelia Plath tells us in *Letters Home*, his "Germanic theory that the man should be *der Herr des Hauses* (head of the house) persisted" (*L*, 13). On the day Sylvia was born, as her mother relates, he announced that " 'I hope for one more thing in life—a son, two and a half years from now.' Warren was born April 27, 1935, only two hours off schedule, and Otto was greeted by his colleagues as 'the man who gets what he wants when he wants it' " (*L*, 12). As his young family grew, Otto Plath's academic career flourished; shortly after Sylvia's birth he published the book *Bumblebees and Their Ways*, and for the first four years of Sylvia's life he devoted much time to scholarly writing, excluding nearly any possibility for social life. As part of his interest in entomology, however, he did keep bees, an activity later pursued by his daughter. A number of her poems, indeed, commemorate this common interest of father and daughter; these are the so-called bee poems of the late volume *Ariel* ("The Bee Meeting," "The Arrival of the Bee Box," "Stings," "The Swarm," and "Wintering") and the *Colossus* poem "The Beekeeper's Daughter."

In 1936 the family moved to the ocean, to Winthrop, Massachusetts. Otto's health had begun to fail, but having diagnosed his illness as lung cancer, Otto refused to see a doctor. He drove himself to continue teaching, and his health deteriorated further. If this was a difficult time at home for Sylvia, it was also a wondrous time for her near the sea. Because her father required much rest and quiet, Sylvia spent many hours at the beach, exploring by herself, playing with her brother or with neighbors, or visiting her maternal grandparents, who lived nearby on the ocean at Point Shirley. Later in her life, Plath was to recall these early seaside years in the settings of many of her poems ("Point Shirley," "Suicide off Egg Rock," and "The Hermit at Outermost House," for example) and to write about them specifically in the autobiographical sketch "Ocean 1212-W" (her grandparents' telephone number), re-creating the sights, sounds, and smells of the oceanside that made such an indelible impression on both her early and her later life.

On the day before Sylvia's 10th birthday, in 1942, the family moved away from the sea. Two years earlier, Otto Plath had died, a victim of diabetes mellitus. Because he had refused medical attention for three years after becoming ill, his malady was correctly diagnosed too late to save his life. Aurelia Plath had found it necessary to return to work to support her family and, despite health problems of her own, had been teaching nearby. Sylvia meanwhile had developed sinusitis, and Warren bronchitis. So, in the summer of 1942, when Aurelia Plath was offered the job of designing and teaching a course in medical secretarial procedures at Boston University, the whole family—Sylvia, Warren, and Aurelia Plath, and Sylvia's maternal grandparents, the Schobers—left the ocean and moved to Wellesley, Massachusetts. There, while Sylvia went to school and her mother went to work, her grandfather found employment and her grandmother took charge of the housework.

## The Wellesley Years: Developing Habits

Sylvia Plath's eight years in Wellesley marked a time of growth and development, a time when writing and academic achievement became increasingly important to her. She was a bright child, an A student; when she moved to Wellesley, she was initially placed in the sixth grade, two years ahead of her chronological peers (her mother had her moved back to fifth). She continued her piano lessons, begun in Winthrop when she was seven, and began to study the viola. She joined the Girl Scouts and attended a Girl Scout camp on Cape Cod for several summers. During the years when she attended the Wellesley public grammar, junior high, and senior high schools, her precocity, so apparent throughout her later career, became increasingly evident. As her mother observed in *Letters Home*, "It was in junior high that she developed work habits and skill in her favorite fields of endeavor, art and writing, winning prizes from the 'scholastic awards' competitions each year" (*L*, 31). Finally, just before leaving for college, Sylvia was awarded a new and long-sought prize; after numerous rejections, her first story, "And Summer Will Not Come Again," was published in the August 1950 issue of *Seventeen*. And in the following November, the same magazine published her poem "Ode on a Bitten Plum."

During her Wellesley years, Sylvia Plath's activities and accomplishments reveal her as a bright, happy, and successful person. Yet her very success bred problems that were both to threaten her equilibrium later in her life and to manifest themselves in her writing. Feeling keenly divided by the apparently incompatible social and intellectual roles she was asked to play, she developed for herself a social mask, establishing the duality of self so evident in the speakers of *The Bell Jar* and her later poetry. As her mother notes, "Sylvia was conscious of the prejudice boys built up among themselves about 'brainy' girls. By the time she was a senior in high school, she had learned to hide behind a façade of light-hearted wit when in a mixed group," so that her greatest joy was not being believed by a date to whom she laughingly revealed that she was a straight-A student (*L*, 38). At the same time, recalls her mother, Sylvia's writing began to reveal "an examination and analysis of the darker recesses of self." This direction, according to Mrs. Plath, is explained by Sylvia's discovery that "problem" literature sold better than "exuberant, joyous outbursts" (*L*, 35, 36).

Another problem bred by—and also no doubt responsible for—Sylvia Plath's accomplishments during this period was Sylvia's setting impossibly high goals for herself. "I want, I think, to be omniscient," she wrote. "I think I would like to call myself 'the girl who wanted to be God.' Yet if I were not in this body, where would I be—perhaps I am *destined* to be classified and qualified. But, oh, I cry out against it" (*L*, 40). Certainly many idealistic, intelligent 17-year-olds have expressed similar sentiments. But in Sylvia Plath they signal the perfectionist attitude that drove her to succeed at the same time that it ensured failure, breeding a kind of destructive energy that was to become increasingly evident in her writing. As she observes, "I have erected in my mind an image of myself—idealistic and beautiful. Is not that image, free from blemish, the true self—the true perfection? Am I wrong when this image insinuates itself between me and the merciless mirror? . . . Never, never will I reach the perfection I long for with all my soul—my paintings, my poems, my stories—all poor, poor reflections" (*L*, 40).

## Smith College: Brilliance and Breakdown

Although her personal and professional accomplishments had become a source not only of satisfaction but also of frustration, Plath continued her well-established habit of award and prize winning. In September 1950 she entered Smith College, the recipient of financial aid from the Nielson Scholarship, the Smith Club of Wellesley, and the Olive Higgins Prouty Fund. Delighted and inspired by the challenging and fertile atmosphere she found there, she thrived both socially and academically. She continued, however, to have difficulty integrating the two; she needed, she said, to "unobtrusively do well in all my courses" (*L*, 48). But if Plath's self-image continued to fall short of the perfection she desired, she managed to affect a "nonbrainy" appearance while appearing vibrant and confident to others. One of her roommates, Nancy Hunter Steiner, describes Sylvia's "clothes and manner" as "deliberately cultivated to disguise any distinction. . . . Sylvia was a remarkably attractive young woman. She was impressively tall, almost statuesque, and she carried the height with an air of easy assurance. . . . The face was angular and its features strong."[2]

Plath continued to write poems and stories and to send them off to publishers. Aurelia Plath at this time became Sylvia's part-time agent and typist, providing for her daughter the encouragement and clerical assistance Aurelia had previously offered her husband. Such support at once lent impetus to Sylvia's career and increased her anxiety, for she now felt driven to succeed in order to reward not only herself but also her mother. "I hope," she wrote to her mother, "I can continue to lay more laurels at your feet" (*L*, 94). But Sylvia also sensed the threat posed by her mother's efforts. Writing to her brother, Sylvia observed that their mother "is an abnormally altruistic person, and I have realized lately that we have to fight against her selflessness as we would fight against a deadly disease." But she continues, "After extracting her life blood and care for 20 years, we should start bringing in big dividends of joy for her" (*L*, 112, 113).

Whatever the source of her inspiration, Plath continued to fare brilliantly in her writing and in her schoolwork. She enjoyed increasing success with prizes and with publication, especially in *Mademoiselle*, *Seventeen*, and *Harper's* magazines. She became an honors student. Any hint of professional, social, or academic rejection spelled failure to her, but generally she seemed able to cope, realizing the therapeutic value of hope and humor. One should, she observed, "*never* . . . commit suicide, because something unexpected always happens." And, "in spite of everything, I still have my good old sense of humor" (*L*, 58, 90).

Among her most cherished prizes was the *Mademoiselle* guest editorship she was awarded for the summer of 1953. In June, along with 19 other college women, Plath went to New York to produce the annual *Mademoiselle* college issue. She was assigned to be managing editor (a disappointment, because she had hoped to be fiction editor), and her duties included interviews with Elizabeth Bowen and with several poets (among them Richard Wilbur and George Steiner) for her "Poets on Campus" feature. New York itself, along with the social activities planned for her group, offered a new, exciting, and bewildering experience. She felt at once stimulated and disoriented, so that sometimes, she confessed in a letter to her brother, "I can't think logically about who I am or where I am going. I have been very ecstatic, horribly depressed, shocked, elated, enlightened, and enervated" (*L*, 117). At the end of June she left for Boston exhausted and depressed. "I will let you know what train my coffin will come in on" (*L*, 120), she wrote her brother.

Plath's experience in New York and the events of the following six months are compellingly portrayed in her autobiographical novel, *The Bell Jar*. Returning home, she learned of her rejection from a fiction-writing class at Harvard summer school; her depression and sense of failure intensified. She tried to learn shorthand, she tried to read, but she could not concentrate. Her mother sought psychiatric help for Sylvia, which resulted in a series of bungled shock treatments. Finally, in August, after leaving a note saying that she had gone for a walk, Sylvia crawled under her house and swallowed a large number of sleeping pills. Three days later she was discovered there and rushed to a hospital. Unable to cope and, as she believed, unable to live up to others' expectations of her, she had attempted suicide. Her act, she told her mother, was "my last act of love" (*L*, 125–26).

She recovered in a private hospital suggested by her faithful benefactress, Olive Higgins Prouty. Her doctor understood her difficulty; as Mrs. Prouty wrote to Sylvia's mother, "Dr. B. suggested that she is a perfectionist, which accounts for her self-depreciation if she falls short of perfection in anything she does" (*L*, 128). By December, Sylvia felt emotionally and physically strong enough to plan a return to Smith for the second semester—as she observes in *The Bell Jar*, "patched, retreaded and approved for the road."[3]

Plath's last three semesters were marked by the same activity and success that had marked her first three college years. She wrote and published more poems and stories, attended Harvard summer school on scholarship, and received several new awards and prizes. Her English honors thesis, on the literary treatment of the double, provides an interesting gloss to her later poetic imagery and personae. Her reading, she reported, included "fascinating stuff about the ego as symbolized in reflections (mirror and water), shadows, twins—dividing off and becoming an enemy, or omen of death, or a warning conscience, or a means by which one denies the power of death (e.g., by creating the idea of the soul as the deathless double of the mortal body)" (*L*, 146).

In June 1955 Plath graduated summa cum laude from Smith and—having received a Fulbright fellowship to Cambridge University—prepared to depart for England.

## Branching Out: Career and Marriage

The seven years that followed marked a period of great activity and promise in Plath's life. It was a time of awakening and maturation, a time filled with experiences both new and momentous to the course of her personal and professional development. In these years, Plath traveled widely; for a time, she wrote more prolifically than ever before; and she married.

In England, during her two years as a Fulbright scholar at Newnham College, Cambridge, Plath continued to enjoy academic achievement and success. In addition to writing regularly and reading for her examination, she joined the university's Dramatic Society, modeled and wrote for the Cambridge newspaper *Varsity*, vacationed in France, and maintained an active social life. In March 1956 Sylvia met the British poet Ted Hughes, and on the following June 16, Bloomsday, they were married. They traveled to Spain for the summer, renting rooms in Benidorm, a small Mediterranean village. There, with her new husband, Plath began to establish an important daily routine to allow her sufficient time for the writing that had become for her a daily necessity.

Returning to Cambridge in the fall, the Hugheses rented an apartment near Grantchester. Sylvia resumed her studies at Newnham while Ted taught at a boys' school. As important as her own writing was to her, Sylvia now apparently initiated the practice of professional deference to her husband. Like her mother before her, Sylvia became typist and agent for someone she loved, devoting much time and energy distributing Ted's poems to potential publishers. About the 1957 publication of his first volume of poetry, she wrote, "I am more happy than if it was my book published! I have worked so closely on these poems of Ted's and typed them so many countless times through revision after revision that I feel ecstatic about it all. I am so happy *his* book is accepted *first*. . . . I can rejoice, then, much more, knowing Ted is ahead of me" (*L*, 297).

Nonetheless, Plath did find time in that year for her own work as well and, in addition to supporting her husband's budding career, published a number of stories and poems in such journals as *Poetry*, *Atlantic*, and the Cambridge magazine *Granta*. In May she took her examinations, in which she excelled. By this time, the Hugheses were ready to move on. Ted had felt increasingly burdened by his teaching duties, which deprived him of the time and energy he preferred to spend in writing. Sylvia, who was eager to return to America, therefore accepted

a job teaching freshman English at Smith College; and the Hugheses
sailed for New York in June 1957.

Back in Northampton, Sylvia experienced frustration similar to Ted's
in the previous year: her teaching left too little time for her writing. And
so, when the school year ended, the Hugheses moved to Boston. They
rented a small Beacon Hill apartment, planning to support themselves
by their writing as best they could. To supplement their income, Sylvia
held several part-time jobs; she worked in a hospital and in a psychia-
trist's office, experiences that provided material for her stories "The
Daughters of Blossom Street" and "Johnny Panic and the Bible of
Dreams." She also attended Robert Lowell's poetry class at Boston University, where she came to know other young poets, among them Anne
Sexton and George Starbuck.

After one year in Boston, however, in the summer of 1959, the
Hugheses planned a return to England. Ted had been awarded a Gug-
genheim grant for the next year's writing; furthermore, he wished for
the child whom he and Sylvia were planning to be born in his native
land. Before leaving the United States, Sylvia and Ted toured the country, traveling first to California to visit Sylvia's paternal aunt, Frieda;
then spending the months of September and October in the writers'
colony at Yaddo, New York, where Sylvia wrote many of her *Colossus*
poems. After a Thanksgiving spent in Wellesley with Sylvia's mother,
the Hugheses departed for London.

In December 1959 Sylvia and Ted settled into a small flat near
Regent's Park. They spent the winter writing, reading, and developing
new friendships; early in 1960 Sylvia signed a contract with William
Heinemann for her first poetry volume, *The Colossus and Other Poems*, and
Ted's second volume was published. On April 1, 1960, Frieda Rebecca
Hughes was born. Although the birth of her first child was wonderful to
her, Plath found the following year increasingly difficult. Her duties as
mother, wife, and secretary left her little time to write, and the submissive conjugal role she accepted contributed to a growing sense of personal unfulfillment.

To most of their new friends, Sylvia was merely Ted's wife. As one of
these friends, A. Alvarez, later observed, "Sylvia seemed effaced, the
poet taking a back seat to the young mother and housewife."[4] Although
Plath cultivated this identity, she also disliked it. She longed for friends
of her own; "I have so missed a good American girl friend!" she wrote
(*L*, 383). Ted's career flourished. He maintained a study away from their
small apartment, at the homes of various neighbors and friends, where

he could write regularly; he gave readings, published prolifically, won many prizes, and achieved increasing recognition. Sylvia, meanwhile, commented: "I really hunger for a study of my own out of hearing of the nursery where I could be alone with my thoughts for a few hours a day" (*L*, 392). She was able to write little, and *The Colossus and Other Poems*, published in November, won no prize and received little publicity. To add to her troubles, Plath's health was poor. In the winter, her sinusitis recurred and she developed appendicitis. Pregnant for the second time, she miscarried in early February 1961, and she had an appendectomy later in the month.

The spring, however, brought a renewal of personal and professional promise. Plath at last located a study of her own and resumed her writing, working on, among other things, *The Bell Jar*. She signed a long-term contract for her poems with the *New Yorker* in March, and in May she received the good news that Alfred A. Knopf planned to publish *The Colossus* in America. She became pregnant again, and she and her husband decided to move to more spacious quarters in the country, where the children could grow and where each parent could have a private study. In September 1961 they bought an ancient, thatch-roofed manor house in Devon, an hour's drive from the sea.

## The Final Years

For a time, life in their new country home proved fruitful and rewarding. The Hugheses established a writing schedule, enabling Sylvia to write in the morning and Ted to write in the afternoon. Plath edited an anthology of American poets for the *Critical Quarterly* and in November was awarded a year's Saxton grant to write poetry. Nicholas Farrar Hughes was born in January 1962. In May, *The Colossus* was published in America, and in June, Plath's voice play, "Three Women," was accepted for the BBC Third Programme. In June Sylvia also began keeping bees.

But by summer, new trouble appeared. The Hughes marriage had begun to fail. As Sylvia's mother observed during a June 1962 visit to Devon, "the marriage was seriously troubled, and there was a great deal of anxiety in the air. Ted had been seeing someone else" (*L*, 458). By summer's end, Ted had moved to London, and Sylvia had initiated arrangements for an agreement of legal separation, to be followed by divorce.

Alone in Devon with her two children, Plath was alternately depressed and hopeful, but always busy. She learned to ride (on her horse named Ariel) and looked forward to adjusting to her new freedom.

She wrote voluminously, between four and eight every morning, composing, as she said, "a poem a day before breakfast. . . . Terrific stuff as if domesticity had choked me" (*L*, 466). At this time, *The Bell Jar* was accepted for publication; she began work on a second novel and anticipated writing a third. In October she observed that "I am writing the best poems of my life" (*L*, 468). By December, she had completed 30 poems, which she saw as her second volume.

Ill health, however, plagued her throughout the fall; she suffered recurrent trouble with the flu and with high fever. And she grew to feel increasingly isolated in Devon: "Stuck down here, as into a sack, I fight for air and freedom and the culture and libraries of a city" (*L*, 465). The bell jar had begun to descend again. She planned, therefore, a restorative vacation in Ireland near the sea later in the winter, to be followed by a move to London where she could continue her work in a livelier cultural environment.

"I am fighting now," Plath observed in October, "against hard odds and alone" (*L*, 469). Difficult though it was, she continued the fight. Abandoning her plans for Ireland, she moved in December to London. The flat she found there was near the place she had shared with her husband a year and a half earlier, but it held great promise for her. It was in W. B. Yeats's former house, and she considered it an ideal place for personal rejuvenation and continued professional success. Although her health was not completely restored and the London winter was unusually cold, Plath maintained the pace she had established for herself, decorating her new apartment and working on her *Ariel* poems in the early morning. She began to gain growing professional recognition in her own right; she made several BBC broadcasts and planned to do more, had new poems accepted for publication, did some reviewing, and planned several poetry readings.

She seemed, for a time, to be winning her fight. "The next five years of my life look heavenly," she wrote in December 1962—"school terms in London, summer in Devon" (*L*, 490). But the odds against her must have seemed too great. On the morning of February 11, 1963, she ended her life by breathing gas from her kitchen oven.

## Chapter Two

# The Biographies: *"Ich Weiss Nicht Wie Soll Es Bedeuten"*

How then shall a biographer paint the life and death of Sylvia Plath, filling in details, making assessments, drawing conclusions? For as writer and biographer Janet Malcolm points out, "in a world of nonfiction we almost never know the truth of what happened. The ideal of unmediated reporting is regularly achieved only in fiction, where the writer faithfully reports on what is going on in his imagination."[1] Nevertheless, there are now five biographies of Plath: Edward Butscher, *Sylvia Plath: Method and Madness* (1976); Linda W. Wagner-Martin, *Sylvia Plath: A Biography* (1987); Anne Stevenson, *Bitter Fame: A Life of Sylvia Plath* (1989); Paul Alexander, *Rough Magic: A Biography of Sylvia Plath* (1991); and Ronald Hayman, *The Death and Life of Sylvia Plath* (1991). There are as well two other studies that, although not biographies in the conventional sense, maintain close intertextual ties to the five biographies: Jacqueline Rose, *The Haunting of Sylvia Plath* (1991) and Janet Malcolm, *The Silent Woman: Sylvia Plath and Ted Hughes* (1994).

These seven works (Butscher, Wagner-Martin, Stevenson, Alexander, Hayman, Rose, and Malcolm), read in order of publication, constitute a complex and fascinating narrative. The five biographies give us what their authors take to be the "real" Sylvia Plath, each promulgating its own view: in general, Butscher is uncharitable to Plath, representing her as conniving and manipulative; Wagner-Martin, Alexander, and Hayman are sympathetic to Plath, portraying her as a victim of social convention, of men, of the expectations of others, and of her own personality and emotional difficulties; and Stevenson, sympathetic to Hughes, returns to the opposing view, depicting Plath as difficult, rapacious, and self-indulgent. In the two most recent studies, Rose evaluates Plath's revelation of herself in her texts, and Malcolm analyzes the requirements and impulses of biography in general and of Plath's case specifically.

Edward Butscher's biography is the first. The Sylvia Plath he draws for us is a divided personality, a "bitch goddess" who is deceptive, affected, and power-hungry. The key to her character, he contends, lies in her college years when, although "not yet schizophrenic in any medical sense, she was three persons, three Sylvias in constant struggle with one another for domination." He describes these warring personalities as

> Sylvia the modest, bright, dutiful, hard-working, terribly efficient child of middle-class parents and strict Calvinist values who was grateful for the smallest favor; Sylvia the poet, the golden girl on campus who was destined for great things in the arts and glittered when she walked and talked; and Sylvia the bitch goddess, aching to go on a rampage of destruction against all those who possessed what she did not and who made her cater to their whims.[2]

It is Butscher's thesis that Plath, a woman of many masks, finally sheds her other identities to become the pure "bitch goddess" at the end of her life, so that the process of refining her art was a process of "translating the bitch goddess into artifice" (Butscher, 264). As one might guess, he takes Ted Hughes's side in discussing the failed marriage, commenting, among other things, on "the 'typical' male desire for freedom from sexual constraints." "Ted," Butscher concludes, "has been roundly, and unfairly, condemned for his 'betrayal' of Sylvia . . . . The future alone can supply a broader and possibly more equitable perspective" (325).

In the immediate "future" is Linda W. Wagner-Martin's biography, published 11 years after Butscher's, and the "perspective" here does seem "more equitable," although probably not in the way Butscher imagines. Wagner-Martin's perspective is also "broader" because primary material is available for her work that was not available to Butscher. Since neither Ted nor Olwyn Hughes (Ted's sister, who was at the time literary executor of Plath's estate) sanctions Wagner-Martin's biography, however, Wagner-Martin works without information the estate might have provided. Using the plentiful materials otherwise available to her, Wagner-Martin creates an evaluation that is sympathetic to Plath and that seems appropriately and accurately based on the evidence. In contrast with Butscher's handling of certain information, Wagner-Martin's approach is less condemnatory and inferential. We can glimpse her method at work in the careful attributions within her account of the marital difficulties between Plath and Hughes:

> He [Ted] called her a 'hag' in a world of beautiful women. He described himself as being dragged down by her—or so Sylvia's letters say. Her correspondence with her mother and with Mrs. Prouty recounts incredible happenings: jealous and angry insults; a fight between Ted and David

Wevill. In the case of Plath's earlier letters, one can compare this correspondence with her private journals to discern the truth. However, the journals from this period of her later life have disappeared—according to Ted Hughes—so comparing accounts is impossible. In her own mind, certainly, Sylvia saw her position as bleak and thought of herself as Ted's victim.[3]

Wagner-Martin gives us a Plath who is by turns intense, angry, and tender, plagued by fears, conflicts, and deep insecurities. She sees in Plath two "dominant personality traits: her tendency to place great weight on something scheduled to happen in the future (and then to be disappointed when it failed to meet her expectations) and a corresponding harshness in her assessment of her own abilities" (Wagner-Martin, 120). These conflicting inclinations, Plath's unceasing hope followed by disappointment, not only produced but perpetuated Plath's difficulties, Wagner-Martin argues; for Plath, each new life event was an adventure, a "new fantasy," yet each failed to meet her unrealistic expectations because of her "tendency to idealize circumstances" (193, 225).

Anne Stevenson's biography, published two years after Linda Wagner-Martin's, seems meant to correct Wagner-Martin's position. In this biography, as in the others, we can find a hint of the author's partiality even before we read the main part of the text, by noticing the author's prefatory description of the working relationship between herself and the Plath estate. Here is part of Stevenson's "Author's Note": "In writing this biography, I have received a great deal of help from Olwyn Hughes, literary agent to the Estate of Sylvia Plath. Ms. Hughes's contributions to the text have made it almost a work of dual authorship. . . ." Stevenson's preface further defines her approach: her aim, she writes, is to confront "some of the misunderstandings generated by [Plath's] meteoric rise to fame, replacing them, as far as possible, with an objective account" of her life and work.[4] "Until now," Stevenson notes, "a whole side of [Plath's] story—that of her marriage—has been inadequately or erroneously presented," and "much of the new material will surprise those who have accepted the current view of Sylvia Plath . . . 'as the pathetic victim of [Ted Hughes's] heartless mistreatment' " (Stevenson, xii). Whether or not Stevenson's account is indeed "objective," her biography does enrich and add dimension to the narrative of Plath's life. Because Stevenson is the first biographer to benefit from Olwyn Hughes's assistance, *Bitter Fame* offers insight and provides information not available elsewhere. The Sylvia Plath whom Stevenson describes is plagued by "existential anxiety," "compulsive orderliness" and "profound terror of an inner chaos she constantly suppressed," "tense, vulnerable nerves," and "paranoia" (4, 101, 109, 131). One cause of her emotional difficulty is her nationality, her American belief in "an inevitable ascension from the discarded past into 'better days' of the future," a "philosophy" that "is childlike, American to the core" (120). She is "egotistical, . . . not because her ego was strong, but because it was perilously weak" (164). She is haughty, has "scant sympathy for lesser mortals," and "took pride in acting the prima donna throughout her life" (123, 125). She is promiscuous until she settles down with Ted: "Mrs. Sylvia Hughes was indeed quite a different person from the garish, sexually rapacious man-chaser of her first terms [at Cambridge]" (101). Even her college boyfriends before Ted had noted "that something in Sylvia was not quite 'right' " (27).

Stevenson's (and Olwyn Hughes's?) bias also reveals itself in denigrating asides, parenthetical remarks, and speculative commentary. Concerning Plath's discomfort at returning to Smith as a faculty member, Stevenson writes that "whatever grounds existed for her paranoia were, *of course*, magnified by her imagination" (114, emphasis added). Plath's thought of having her mother spend her retirement in England is dismissed as Sylvia's "*angling* for a babysitter as well as for a supportive mother" (248, emphasis added). Stevenson further attributes to Plath impulses and motivations that seem, at best, speculation. (Or, more mysteriously, we wonder whether such comments represent the veiled view of Olwyn and/or Ted Hughes.) For example: "Sylvia could not resist a gratuitous dig" at a neighbor (135). "Ted Hughes must have begun to feel himself trapped under the same doomed bell jar" (239). "These [late] poems . . . are bereft of all normal 'human' feeling. . . . The result is an unfurling, perhaps unique in poetry, of 'unpoetic' negative emotions of an extreme kind" (270).

In the case of Hughes's alliance with Assia Wevill, Plath seems portrayed as unilaterally responsible for the affair. Stevenson's sources, where they are identified, are Assia herself in conversation with others: "Assia later gave Olwyn Hughes much the same account . . . and remarked that she doubted whether the attraction between Ted and herself would ever have developed into an affair, as it later did, had Sylvia behaved differently." Previously, "Assia confided to Suzette Macedo that Sylvia had picked up 'a current of attraction' between Assia and Ted and had reacted badly" (243, 243–44). Because subsequent events confirmed Plath's suspicions, one might ask what is a "bad" reaction? And is Assia the best judge of Sylvia in this matter? In the failure of the Plath-Hughes marriage, writes Stevenson, "Ted's adultery" is not "the critical issue"; rather, "the inflexibility of [Sylvia's] self-absorption, coupled with the dark moods that were inseparable from her strange genius, may finally have broken down her husband's defenses" (257).

The next two biographies, published two years after Stevenson's, appear meant to refute Stevenson's portrait of Plath and, once again, to draw a sympathetic picture. Paul Alexander chooses *Rough Magic* for his epigraph and title, words from Prospero's closing monologue in *The Tempest*: "But this rough magic / I here abjure . . ." Alexander's title is rich with meaning and ambiguity; the reference to Prospero's relinquishment of his magical powers suggests Plath's suicidal surrender of the magical power of her art. Prospero's other words, given in Alexander's epigraph, clearly echo Plath's poetic language and personal concerns: "Bury it certain fathoms" and "I'll drown my book." Plath is not only Prospero but also Ariel, the captive spirit with whom Plath so clearly identified herself. Alexander's epigraph and title, especially the phrase "rough magic," may be intended to point as well to his characterization of Ted Hughes as "rough" in both tangible and intangible ways and as a disciple of magic, casting Hughes as Prospero and Plath again as Ariel.

Alexander's preface signals his approach:

> Historically, when an author has submitted a manuscript to the Plath estate for permission to quote, the Hugheses have asked the author for changes in substance as well as quotation in exchange for that permission. I decided early on that I would not subject myself to the constraints of the estate, and so I did not quote from unpublished sources . . . . I also determined that I would not quote so extensively from published material that I would have to seek permission from the estate.[5]

With many sources still available to him, however, Alexander writes a chatty, informative narrative. His technique enhances the inferential character of his style, for he acknowledges his sources not within the text but in page notes at the end of the book. A story therefore emerges that seems Alexander's own, portraying Plath as a victim of her own clinical depression, of her past, and of her adulterous husband. And Ted Hughes receives the most negative depiction found within these biographies.

Using an analytic approach, Alexander contributes new data to the growing biographical narrative. Plath's readers, for example, are well aware of the deleterious effect on Plath's psyche of her shock treatments, but Alexander explains their special difficulty for Plath by placing her experience in a medical-historical context:

> In later years, standard medical procedure would demand that doctors administer electroshock therapy only after the patient was given a muscle relaxant and a general anesthetic. Also, a doctor or a nurse would stay with the patient during the recovery period, to provide support and counseling. In the case of Sylvia Plath none of this happened. Because she had taken no muscle relaxant, her body was rigid with fear. Because she had received no anesthesia, she was, in effect, nearly electrocuted. Because no doctor or nurse accompanied her in recovery, she experienced a painful, numbing loneliness as she lay on the table by herself . . . [so that] her anxiety *increased* with electroshock therapy. (Alexander 1991, 120)

Alexander also locates Plath's emotional difficulties not in her temperament, as other biographers do, but in her genetic history. After Plath's "release from McLean," he reveals, "Aurelia received word from one of Otto's sisters that in the Plath family, their mother, a sister, and a niece all suffered from depression" and that "Otto's mother had become so sick that she had been hospitalized. Perhaps Sylvia's illness did not result from outside factors at all. Perhaps she had simply inherited the disease from her father" (Alexander 1991, 135).

In the fifth biography, Ronald Hayman's *The Death and Life of Sylvia Plath*, we see once more the sympathetic tilt in using sources and interpreting information (in this case, again toward Plath). Hayman states his intent to reply to the Stevenson biography, which was "most informative" yet "has little to say about [Plath's] death" by "help[ing] to correct some of the imbalance created by writers who have been unfair to Sylvia Plath."[6] But we see in Hayman's book the beginning of a new trend in this intertextual biographical narrative: the use of analytical perspective rather than biographical narrative as an organizing principle. It is Hayman's aim not only to inform and interpret but also, as his title suggests, to rearrange his discussion of Plath's life, to help us "understand Sylvia Plath's life" by "understanding the long relationship with death which was eventually consummated in suicide" (Hayman, xiii).

Hayman frames his account of Plath's "Death and Life" as a mystery story, raising several intriguing questions in his opening chapter: "One of the mysteries that still surrounds her death is what happened to the

Morris station wagon"; a solution to that puzzle might help "to establish whether the man she was planning to meet then was the man who turned up at the inquest, and whether it was Hughes she was expecting to see on Sunday night" (Hayman, 17). There are also the mysteries of the missing suicide note, the missing keys, the missing will, the missing letter to Aurelia Plath, the missing journals, and the missing novel. Hayman piques our curiosity with these mysteries in his first chapter and returns to them in his last one; disappointingly, however, he solves none of them.

Hayman focuses on Plath's death, a suicide, he contends, "that was designed not to fail" and that had multiple causes. "In so far as her suicide was an act of aggression, it was aimed against [Hughes] and his new lover, Assia Wevill" (Hayman, 14, 93). If Plath knew of Assia's pregnancy, which had been confirmed before Plath's death, "it would have been in character" for the "unscrupulous" Assia "to inflict the triumphant news of her pregnancy on her defeated rival, and if she did, this may have been a factor in Sylvia's decision to die" (197). An additional contributing factor, theorizes Hayman, was Plath's inability to think clearly because of the drugs she was taking. "She was obviously exceeding the [recommended] dosage," which "may well have been the cause of the slurred vowels, the faraway look and the seraphic expression" observed by witnesses (194).

Hayman also provides an informative final chapter containing details about Plath's family in the years after her death. Here we read more about Assia, about Hughes's infidelity to her, and about Hughes's other women. Hayman also contributes a thorough posthumous publication history. And, at the beginning of the book, he supplies a detailed and useful chronology.

Jacqueline Rose's *The Haunting of Sylvia Plath* completes the shift away from biographical narrative and toward what we might call biographical-textual analysis. Rose announces in her preface that her "focus is on writing," particularly on "the way it has been edited, presented and read." Indeed, Rose declares that her book is not a biography. "I am never claiming to speak about the life, never attempting to establish the facts about the lived existence of Sylvia Plath . . . because accounts of the life . . . have to base themselves on a spurious claim to knowledge, they have to arbitrate between competing and often incompatible versions of what took place."[7]

Like other writers before her, Rose has apparently run afoul of Plath's estate, "the demands" on her in her interpretation of certain poetry having "become more and more restrictive and impossible to meet," especially because "it appears that for Ted and Olwyn Hughes there is only one version of reality, one version—their version—of the truth." Recognizing "how distressing the situation is for all those who were, and who become, involved in Plath's work," Rose nevertheless offers what she calls "one reading of the work of Sylvia Plath, one part of a story that has clearly not come to an end" (Rose, xi, xii). It is not Rose's intention, however, to "pass judgement on the issue of Plath's pathology" as other biographers do, because she does "not believe we can take writing as unproblematic evidence for the psychological condition or attributes of the one who writes" (4). Rose's study will grow from "the extent to which she haunts me" (10).

What follows is a deconstructive reading that focuses on the ways "Plath regularly unsettles certainties of language, identity and sexuality" and on "the play of gender, sexuality and power in the writing of Sylvia Plath" (xii, 115). For those interested in the shift within the collective narrative of Plath's biographers from recounting and interpreting life events toward analyzing the biographical impulse itself, one of Rose's chapters holds particular interest. As Ronald Hayman's closing chapter addresses the interplay of publication and personality after Plath's death, Rose's chapter "The Archive" extends this account by examining the "abuse" evident in "the control by Ted Hughes of Sylvia Plath's legacy and work" (Rose, 65). Principally "at issue," argues Rose, is "the question of the 'facts,' of who controls them" and of "Hughes's claim to speak for" them (66). Although Hughes may be the main "editing, controlling, and censoring presence," however, he is not "the only person involved in this process of editing, censoring, attempting to direct the interpretation of, and response to, Plath's work" (70, 74). There are also Olwyn Hughes, Aurelia Plath, the biographers themselves, and Anne Stevenson in particular, who "makes falseness, distortion, perversion, the key characteristic of Plath herself." In light of such conflicting special interests, "to own the facts of one's own life is not self-evidence, it is *war*—a war in which husbands and wives, mothers and daughters battle over the possession of—or rather, the constitution of what will pass *as*—the truth." Yet this war is characterized by "a complexity of motives" that grows from both "self-protection" and "the psychic pain" of "each of these protagonists" (76).

Rose uses Stevenson's biography as an example of "the impossibility of objectivity" (Rose, 97). Calling *Bitter Fame* "something of a '*cause célèbre*' in the genre of abusive biography," Rose argues that one cannot read the image of Plath offered by Stevenson "as anything other than a systematic assault on Plath" and "a vindication of Hughes." Therefore, "reading this book . . . ," one sees how "precisely . . . impossible" it is "to know whom to believe":

> Either you believe [Plath], see her as the aggrieved party, her voice put down in the interests of the one guilty of her distress; or you accept the view of the [Stevenson] biography, discredit her utterance and disbelieve what you have read. If the only sane position is finally to conclude that you do not know, then we should none the less note that this form of sanity is a position which can also drive you mad. (93, 95, 97)

In *The Silent Woman,* published three years after Jacqueline Rose's book, Janet Malcolm, agreeing with Rose about the ultimate impossibility of knowing, points to "the epistemological insecurity by which the reader of biography and autobiography (and history and journalism) is always and everywhere dogged" (Malcolm, 154). Malcolm therefore focuses on the requirements and problems of writing biography in general and on the predicaments of Plath biographers in particular. "Biography," writes Malcolm, "can be likened to a book that has been scribbled in by an alien. After we die, our story passes into the hands of strangers. The biographer feels himself to be not a borrower but a new owner, who can mark and underline as he pleases" (184). And, Malcolm reminds us, such markings will naturally imply a point of view, because "writing cannot be done in a state of desirelessness," and, like other Plath observers, "I, too, have taken a side—that of the Hugheses and Anne Stevenson—and I, too, draw on my sympathies and antipathies and experiences to support it" (177).

Malcolm's purpose, however, is to study not Plath's life itself but the studies of it. In pursuing that aim, she reports on her reading of Plath's letters and journals and on meetings with Ted and Olwyn Hughes, Anne Stevenson, A. Alvarez, Jacqueline Rose, and other Plath acquaintances. She also evaluates the Plath biographies, noting (among other things) the Hughes camp's displeasure with those biographers who "advertised their independence of the Plath estate" by failing to request "permission to quote from Plath's writings" and who "with their paraphrases and interviews with hostile witnesses" have "raised Hughes's punishment by biography to a new level of excruciation" (165). Of the five biographies, Malcolm (not surprisingly, given her partiality) finds Stevenson's "by far the most intelligent and the only [one that is] aesthetically satisfying" (10). Surely, says Malcolm, "if Hughes was indeed speaking about his marriage to Plath through Stevenson this might add to the biography's value, not decrease it" (12). Paradoxically, the very reasons that permit Malcolm's praise of Stevenson's work allow others' condemnation of it.

So we come finally to the impossibility of knowing, and after reading the seven biographical works sequentially, this conclusion is as natural as it is frustrating. Both the pro-Plath and the pro-Hughes positions are well and apparently thoroughly represented within the first five biographies. There remain, of course, a few unsolved mysteries (identified mostly by Hayman), the solution of which might provide a successful sleuth with material for another biography. There is also the hope that additional primary material might appear (the missing journals, or novel, or letters, or more poetry, or whatever), providing data for a new biography. But after the 1991 publication of the fourth and fifth biographies, there seems to have developed a sense of futility in continuing ordinary biographical narrative. Most onlookers have formed their opinions about whether or not Plath was a sympathetic character in the narrative they imagine of her life; most observers sense whether or not they want to approach, use, trust, or avoid the information available from Ted and Olwyn Hughes, depending on the partiality the observers themselves bring to Plath's story; and most readers recognize the sympathies and preferences of other witnesses who had actually known Plath. Rose and Malcolm, therefore, move toward discussing biography rather than writing it.

The "real" Sylvia constructed in Plath's poetry and fiction, letters and journals, remains powerful and ultimately unknowable; each biographer and each reader of the biographies finds the person and poet he or she imagines. There indeed seems no hope, as Jacqueline Rose points out, of resolution or agreement, for "to try to construct a single, consistent image of Plath becomes meaningless" both because of the "vested interests" of so many individuals and because of "the multiplicity of representations that Plath offers of herself" (Rose, 104). In the end, what we can know best is expressed in the words of Heinrich Heine's *The Lorelei* that Plath's mother sang to her as a child: "*Ich weiss nicht wie soll es bedeuten.*" "I don't know what it means." "I don't know what to make of it."

# Chapter Three
# The Journals: Art and Artifice

Finding divergent viewpoints in biographers' portraits of Sylvia Plath, a reader may turn to Plath's journals in search of the real Sylvia, hoping that Plath's own entries will provide additional keys to the interpretive puzzle of her character and temperament. So long as such a reader heeds the nature of the genre, bearing in mind that journalistic narrative is by nature selective and to some degree contrived, she or he will find in *The Journals of Sylvia Plath* valuable insight into Plath's personality and motivations, together with useful information about her work. A reader will also find, however, that like the biographies, the journals are subject to external slanting and selection.

*The Journals of Sylvia Plath*[1] comprise the period from July 1950, before Plath entered Smith College as a freshman, to July 4, 1962, approximately seven months before her suicide. Published in 1982, the volume is copyrighted "by Ted Hughes as the Executor of the Estate" and by Frances McCullough, Plath's editor. Hughes, as "Consulting Editor" copyrights the "text of the journals" and his "Foreword" (*J*, v); McCullough, as "Editor" (*J*, v), copyrights "additional text," which includes her "Editor's Note" (*J*, vi). The plentiful entries of part 1, "Smith College 1950–51"; part 2, "Cambridge 1955–57, Smith College 1957–58"; and the first section of part 3, "Boston 1958–59" are arranged chronologically. The entries for the second section of part 3, "England 1960–62" (the final entries of the journal) are few and are arranged topically. The editors assert that these are *"character sketches"* that come from Plath's notes and that the entries are *"separate from her regular journals and are all that survive in prose from this period, though she was also at work on a second novel"* (*J*, 343–44). (A reader may wonder whether "regular journals" did exist from this period but failed to "survive in prose.")

This volume, then, includes Plath's selected, not complete, journals. As Frances McCullough points out in her "Editor's Note," Plath *"began keeping a diary when she was a child"* and *"kept it right up until her death."* *The Journals'* editors have, however, *"{cut} . . . the work"* according to *"a few basic principles,"* which are *"elements relating to {Plath's} work, her inner*

21

*life, and her valiant struggle to find herself and her voice. This leaves a great deal of material by the road . . ."*; there are *"lots of missing pages of ordinary commentary that seemed not particularly relevant to any of the basic concerns of the book,"* the deletions guided in part by *"concern"* for *"Plath's survivors"* ( *J,* ix). Her juvenile entries are therefore excluded, as are potentially important accounts of her thoughts and feelings in the several years preceding her death in 1963 (some no doubt excised, some ambiguously missing).

## Motifs

Plath discloses her journalistic intentions throughout the volume; her entries evince her aim of keeping track of her joys, hopes, dreams, disappointments, successes, and fears. Her writings, therefore, are full of rumination, contemplation, reflection, and analysis, and they reveal a person who at ages 17 through 29 (July 1950–July 1962) is candid, perceptive, and intelligent. "It is more important to capture moments like this, keen shifts in mood, sudden veerings of direction—than to lose it in slumber," she writes on November 14, 1952 ( *J,* 65). "God, how I ricochet between certainties and doubts," she declares on April 27, 1953 ( *J,* 78). Her entries often demonstrate her awareness of the struggle between intellectual comprehension and emotional jeopardy. For example, preceding her August 1953 suicide attempt, she lectures herself: "You are plunged so deep in your own very private little whirlpool of negativism that you can't do more than force yourself into a rote [of simple action]" ( *J,* 85). "Stop thinking selfishly of razors and self-wounds and going out and ending it all. Your room is not your prison. You are"( *J,* 87).

Other motifs and revelations emerge from this journalistic narrative. Like a tragedian, she explores the concept that "character is fate," as she writes in 1952, "and damn, I'd better work on my character" ( *J,* 64). Elsewhere Plath shows flashes of humor; she muses about writing her "whole novel on the pink, stiff, lovely-textured Smith memorandum pads" ( *J,* 201) or writing "a poem about a fool on April Fool's Day" ( *J,* 214). In a more serious mood, Plath also recognizes and fears her perfectionist tendencies: "Not being perfect hurts," she writes in 1957 while an instructor at Smith ( *J,* 178). Further, she is sometimes prescient, as when she senses at age 19, in her sophomore year at Smith, that she "cannot marry a writer or artist" because the "conflict of egos" would be "dangerous" ( *J,* 74). And later she comprehends the danger of having married one: "If [Ted] weren't my husband," she writes in 1958, "I would have run from him as a killer" (*J*, 219).

In 1950, while a freshman at Smith, Plath analyzes the glib, impertinent tone so familiar in her poetry and fiction: "Because you're still vulnerable, because you still don't have faith in yourself, you talk a little fliply, a little too wisely, just to cover up so you won't be accused of sentimentality or emotionalism or feminine tactics" (*J*, 25). This observation by the 18-year-old Plath is meaningful in several ways. For one thing, Plath recognizes her adoption of this tone as juvenile and defensive. But in later years she becomes master of the tone, refining and transforming it into mature and forceful art. The bold, insolent voice of Lady Lazarus and of other speakers in Plath's late poems fuses teenage defensiveness with adult authority (and fear, and desperation), creating controlled and potent energy. Further, the comment's concluding words ("feminine tactics") indicate Plath's own ambivalent relationship with feminism (a relatively new, or newly revived, movement in 1950). Because Plath's critics debate her stance on this issue, we should note that we can turn to *The Journals* for what seems an accurate record of her position.

The phrase "feminine tactics" is negative in character, and other remarks throughout *The Journals* appear to support such an inclination. In several entries, for example, Plath expresses pleasure in her subservient domestic or inferior professional role: She "love[s] cooking for [Ted] (made a lemon layer cake last night) and being secretary, and all" (*J*, 221). She is "glad Ted is first" (*J*, 154); she is happy about Ted's publishing successes while she still seeks recognition and "would rather have it this way, if either of us was successful." "That's why I could marry him," she writes, "knowing he was a better poet than I" (*J*, 172). One senses that in entries such as these, which appear mostly during her relationship with Hughes, Plath is expressing attitudes internalized by her socialized self: a woman ought to marry, serve her man, embrace domesticity, subjugate herself to her family, and live happily ever after. And one also senses that, rather than expressing a firm conviction, such entries display Plath's attempt to convince herself of the validity of such a viewpoint.

In other entries, indeed, spanning the entire journalistic narrative, a contradictory belief breaks through. "I dislike being a girl," she writes in 1950. "I must pour my energies through the direction and force of my mate" (*J*, 23). In 1951 she asks, "Must I lose [my sensitivity] in cooking scrambled eggs for a man?" (*J*, 33) and complains that her gender curtails her freedom, "being born a woman is my awful tragedy" (*J*, 30).

By 1958, now married to Hughes, she fears her dependence on her husband and dreads getting "sucked into a tempting but disastrous whirlpool" (*J*, 246). In 1959 she comments on the degrading male attitude that "women shouldn't think, shouldn't be unfaithful (but their husbands may be), must stay home, cook, wash" (*J*, 292). In these remarks, Plath expresses her distaste for subordinate female status with its thwarted power and its diminished possibilities. This is a predicament that, according to *The Journals*, Plath never resolves. (One may hope, however, that had Plath lived past her marriage with Hughes and the devastation of its failure, she might have reconnected with her earlier protofeminist reflections, shed some of her domestic, subordinate proclivities, and inclined more strongly toward feminism.)

Her misgivings about the viability of either role, at least, are clearly recorded in her journals. And one related motif that emerges from these journals is the promise and failure of the Cinderella story. From *The Journals'* early pages, Plath is Cinderella, looking for her prince, hoping for his appearance, apprehensive about his arrival, fearful that he will never materialize, overcoming difficulties as she waits. Like Cinderella, too, she is delighted when he does appear, joyful at first in his presence and in the coincidental fulfillment of her dream. But Plath comes gradually to realize (as her doubts about her own role in such a fairy-tale relationship have insinuated) that Cinderella and her prince may actually not live happily after and that this fairy-tale ending does not tell enough. Although Cinderella's marriage to her prince may conclude her story, a real-life marriage must be both an end and a beginning.

This ground is uncharted for Plath, as for Cinderella, and one wonders whether Plath's difficulty in writing this new chapter might grow in some part from the crucial absence of a successful, postnuptial paradigm for Cinderella. One might suggest, as well, that the new chapter Plath does write grows from a cruel and ironic reversal of the fairy-tale model, for in Plath's case the prince turns out to be a frog. One might even conclude that in her later years, Plath, like Anne Sexton in her poem "Cinderella" and in other *Transformations* poems, consciously subverts the Cinderella story, thereby unifying her life and her art. Her late poetry gains artistic power from the collapse of her domestic life.

## Controversial Incidents

*The Journals* do, however, hint at Plath's perspectives on and reactions to certain issues that generate controversy among her biographers. For example, two incidents concerning Plath's friend Jane are cited by biographers unsympathetic to Plath. In one episode, Sylvia and Jane make a short visit to Paris from Cambridge; Jane goes to sleep in their shared hotel room; Sylvia goes out for a walk and, upon returning, finds herself locked out. On another occasion, Jane borrows some of Plath's new textbooks, which Plath has studied and underlined, and Jane writes in her own annotations and underlinings. Some biographers cite Jane's bewilderment at Sylvia's excessive rage at having been locked out of the hotel room and at Jane's having added her writings to Plath's new books, claiming both events as evidence of Plath's pathological anger. Concerning the hotel incident, however, Plath herself exhibits no anger at all in her journal, mentioning the occasion briefly in a playful list of her and her friends' curious behavior (*J*, 99). The book episode receives only brief mention as well (one 5 1/4-line paragraph): Plath says she was "furious" but exhibits no anger at the time of writing the journal entry. Indeed, she seeks to understand Jane's motive, writing that "evidently [Jane] felt that since I'd already underlined [the books] in black, nothing further could harm them" (*J*, 127).

Another episode cited by biographers (unsympathetic to Plath) concerns Plath's sewing of her husband's clothes. These biographers cite Hughes's disclosure to friends, as evidence of his wife's viciousness, that Plath "hide[s] shirts, rip[s] up torn socks, never sew[s] on buttons" (*J*, 277). Yet the quotation just before, because it comes from Plath's own journals, indicates Plath's thorough awareness of what she contends is misrepresentation: "His motive: I thought that would make you do it. So he thought by shaming me, he could manipulate me" (*J*, 277). Is a wife "vicious" who does not sew buttons on her husband's shirts? Does assertion equal viciousness in Plath's husband's view? What is going on here? Whom should we believe?

Again, in her entry of May 19, 1958, Plath writes about what she perceives as her husband's flirtations during her year as an instructor at Smith. On one occasion, according to the journals, when Hughes fails to meet Plath after her final class of the year, she discovers him "coming up the road from Paradise Pond, where girls take their boys to neck on weekends" (*J*, 232); Hughes is smiling and talking earnestly (in a "fatuous, admiration-seeking" way, writes Plath) with an undergraduate whose "eyes souped up giddy applause" (*J*, 233). The student sees Plath and runs away. Pro-Hughes biographers dismiss this episode as evidence of Plath's pathological jealousy; pro-Plath biographers consider it valid evidence of Hughes's womanizing proclivities. Plath herself casts the

incident, reasonably it seems, in the context of her incipient distrust of
her husband.

## Editing

A reader of Plath's *Journals* hopes for more entries that might divulge
Plath's views and feelings about incidents that are widely and contradic-
torily discussed in the biographies and in certain memoirs. Alas, however, such entries are few, for the executors' partialities in working with
the biographers extend to *The Journals* as well. For example, in an inter-
polation preceding Plath's entry of May 19, 1958, the editors prepare us
for reading about Plath's suspicions of her husband during the Smith
College flirtation episodes: *"About this time, . . . Plath began to feel an
upsurge of rage. . . . In the passage that follows it is a rage against her husband
in which a small incident takes on enormous proportions . . ."* ( *J*, 228).

In this and in other ways, *The Journals'* editors supervise Plath's text
throughout. In the "Editor's Note" and "Foreword" to *The Journals*,
Frances McCullough and Ted Hughes stress the autobiographical function of *The Journals "in the absence of a good biography"* (McCullough, *J*, ix)
(remember that Edward Butscher's is the only biography published
before 1982); the editors thereby appear to see themselves partially as
biographers. Certainly, the journals of an artist or a public figure nearly
always provide (auto)biographical insight of some kind, affirming or
correcting or enriching the wider audience's views. Yet in the case of
Plath's journals, there is an indication of marked editorial selection, for
both editors admit that there has been some tinkering with Plath's
manuscripts.

Unfortunately, the sort of tinkering that has taken place, the guiding
principle for excisions and expurgations, is both too vague and too
apparent. As noted above, McCullough comments that *"we have tried, in
the cutting of the work, to stick to a few basic principles"* and *"to include what
seem to us the most important elements,"* and that these standards *"{leave} a
great deal of material by the road"* ( *J*, ix). Clarity would be useful here:
What are "the most important elements"? What kind of "material" has
been left "by the road"? How much is "a great deal"? Some portion of
the answer to these questions lies in McCullough's expressed concern for
Plath's survivors. Another part, however, may reside in McCullough's
further comments that *"There are quite a few nasty bits missing"* ( *J*, ix) and
that *"some of the more devastating comments are missing—these are marked
{omission}"* ( *J*, x). We cannot know what McCullough means by "nasty

bits" and "devastating comments," but this reader, at least, regrets their deletion. Furthermore, when we read sections of *The Journals* that McCullough has decided are not too "nasty," the omissions (whatever they are) seem likely to be either editorially biased or prudish, like bleeps in a television movie.

Similarly, Hughes comments that "This is [Plath's] autobiography, far from complete, but complex and accurate" (*J*, xiii). Although the "whole bulk" of Plath's journals are available at Smith College, he declares, "this selection [*The Journals*] contains perhaps a third" of that whole. But even the "whole bulk" is incomplete, we must realize, for Hughes admits that one notebook, covering a nonspecified period beginning in 1959, "disappeared," and the notebook that followed (presumably covering the period before Plath's death) was "destroyed" because he "did not want her children to have to read it" (*J*, xiii). In his essay "Sylvia Plath and Her Journals," Hughes adds that the "disappeared" journal "may, presumably, still turn up."[2] And in "Time Capsule: 2013," reviewer Edwin McDowell, noting that the Smith journals were formerly "in possession of [Plath's] husband and literary executor, Ted Hughes," reveals that "in certain cases . . . readers will have to make do with expurgated typescripts; portions of the journals that comment on people still living have been sealed until the year 2013."[3]

Hughes's foreword to *The Journals* is apparently "an earl[y], shorter draft" of an essay that Hughes had initially intended to use; Paul Alexander reprints the original, longer essay in his collection *Ariel Ascending*.[4] Some of Hughes's deletions from the longer essay are instructive: What Hughes calls his "motive in publishing these journals" is to provide "firsthand testimony" to counterbalance "the account [Plath] gave of herself in her letters to her mother, or. . . the errant versions supplied by her biographers." Therefore, "these papers, which contain the nearest thing to a living portrait of her, are offered in the hope of providing some ballast for our idea of the reality behind the poems."[5]

Bias seems evident here; the biographers' "versions" are "errant"; the Plath represented in these expurgated journals conforms with "our idea" of her character. The published *Journals*, then, appear to depict the Sylvia Plath that Hughes and McCullough want us to see. Editorial selection, evaluation, and subtle commentary continue throughout *The Journals*: "*Entries from* [Plath's freshman year at Smith] *in the journal are not dated,*" and "*so many cuts have been made in the text that the reader should not be encouraged to attempt to read these excerpts in a close narrative way*" (*J*, 16–17). "*Only the following entry has survived of the Guest Editor experience at* Mademoiselle" ( *J*, 81). *"Journals have disappeared—if they existed—for the two years after Plath's breakdown in the summer of 1953"* ( *J*, 88). *"She kept excerpts from her strange, impassioned letters to Sassoon as part of her journal"* ( *J*, 90). (Whose evaluation is involved in determining what is "strange"?). *"Most of the descriptive material written at the time has a strangely flat quality in retrospect"* ( *J*, 144). (Again, "strangely flat"?) And so on.

Also interjected into Plath's journals, expurgated though they may be, is an editorial description of Plath's *"extremely close and involved relationship"* with her mother, together with a short account of their complex and *"symbiotic, deeply supportive union"* ( *J*, 265). This editorial section is followed immediately by a release from Plath's mother giving "consent" to print the entries about Plath's 1958–1959 psychiatric visits in Boston "in the interest of furthering understanding of [Sylvia's] emotional condition." Mrs. Plath would like us to understand, however, that her daughter's "negative thoughts" are "cancel[ed]" by other, more positive pages, that she finds the material "painful," and that her "decision to approve its release has been difficult" ( *J*, 266). One wonders whether such commentary by a poet's mother and editors belongs in the main text of an artist's published journals. Yet the very ambiguous presence and content of these materials may unwittingly provide hints about the nature of other excluded passages: Did the editors not seek or fail to obtain Mrs. Plath's permission to print them? Are the editors and Mrs. Plath somehow in cahoots? It is possible that the existence of a certain sympathy between Mrs. Plath and the Hughes family before Sylvia's death may reveal something about the sources of the artist's distress. The contrast of the mother's reluctant permission with the daughter's intense, searching self-analysis dramatizes Sylvia Plath's predicament, discloses the nature of at least part of her dilemma, and exhibits the character of her trouble.

Like the biographies, finally, these journals demonstrate the ultimate impossibility of knowing. Like the biographies, *The Journals* slant to promulgate a certain point of view. In each biography, the point of view is plainly the biographer's; in *The Journals*, we are on unsteady ground in deciding to whom the point of view belongs. Have we been given enough of Plath's journals to get a genuine feel for her personality and temperament? It is hard to say, because so many entries, particularly those concerning crucial life events (those speculated upon by her biographers, for example, or those concerning her breakdown, her marriage's failure, or her last months) are missing. Did such entries ever exist? Do they still exist somewhere? Is the character who emerges from these pages Sylvia Plath, or is it Ted Hughes and Frances McCullough's idea of Sylvia Plath? Or is it Sylvia's mother's and/or Hughes's and/or McCullough's notion of Sylvia Plath's proper image for posterity? We can know that *The Journals* editors have tried to manipulate the Plath whom we see. But we can know little else.

For the writing in *The Journals* is narrative, selected and tilted, as is any narrative, by (in this case) the journalist herself, her editors, perhaps her mother, and perhaps others. As Janet Malcolm observes in commenting on the biographical attitude, "the pose of fairmindedness, the charade of evenhandedness, the striking of an attitude of detachment can never be more than rhetorical ruses" (Malcolm, 177). This observation may apply as well to this autobiography; in the expurgated, editorialized *Journals*, "fairmindedness" does seem to be a conscious pretense on the part of Plath's editors. Nor can the journalist herself (nor can anyone), even though Plath may be attempting genuine "fairmindedness" and "evenhandedness," achieve complete objectivity. Finally, *The Journals of Sylvia Plath* must be valued for its writer's art and recognized for its artifice.

## Chapter Four

# Fiction: *The Bell Jar*
# and *Johnny Panic*

### *The Bell Jar*

During 1961 and early 1962, a period both of great personal difficulty and great creative productivity, Sylvia Plath worked on her autobiographical novel, *The Bell Jar*. Even as she wrote it, Plath must have sensed the shock its appearance in print might cause those people whom she had adapted for her fictional use as well as the discomfort its revelations, made public, might bring to her, for she was at once pleased by its acceptance for publication and reticent to accept responsibility for its authorship. In her frequent letters to her mother, she made no mention of her work; in a letter to her brother, she noted its acceptance, but cautioned: "This is a secret; it is a pot-boiler and no one must read it!" (*L*, 472). In January 1963, the novel was published pseudonymously under the name "Victoria Lucas."

Recording a period of confusion, disintegration, and renewal in the life of its protagonist and narrator, Esther Greenwood, *The Bell Jar* draws its materials primarily from the time of Plath's *Mademoiselle* guest editorship, in the summer of 1953, through her subsequent breakdown and attempted suicide, to the time when, sufficiently rehabilitated, she returned to college. The novel no doubt represents an attempt on its author's part to place these turbulent months in mature perspective, for it records Esther Greenwood's struggle to connect knowledge with experience, past with present and future, and desire with reality.

### Disintegration

The subject of Plath's English honors thesis, on which she worked after returning to college in 1954, was the literary treatment of the double. In *The Bell Jar*, Plath not only creates a similar scholarly interest for Esther Greenwood, she also provides fictional realization of the device.

Elly Higginbottom is Esther Greenwood's other self, the embodiment of her fantasy. Esther's dilemma, her "split personality" as she calls it (*B,* 23), is dramatized in the novel's opening chapter by her inability to decide between two potential "best friends." Vacillating between the innocent, wholesome Betsy and the urbane, sexy Doreen, she finds herself unable to form a complete identification with either one because she herself is divided, in a similar way, between conditioning and desire. To express that inner division, Esther Greenwood creates Elly Higginbottom.

Elly Higginbottom tries, like Doreen, to be worldly and sexually sophisticated. Whatever Esther Greenwood is, Elly represents the Other, and at the same time that Elly embodies Esther's wish fulfillment, her otherness is complete. Esther is insecure; Elly is supremely self-confident. Esther lives in Boston, a place where she feels constrained by people like her mother and Mrs. Willard to be sexually proper and conventional; Elly comes from Chicago, a place safely distant, "the sort of place where unconventional, mixed-up people would come from" (*B,* 148). Confesses Esther as she assumes her Elly guise: "I didn't want anything I said or did that night to be associated with me and my real name" (*B,* 13). Thus, Elly can attempt to discard the restraining shyness and social insecurity of Esther and seek pickup dates with Frankie or a Boston sailor. Esther is a scholarship student from a "big eastern women's college" who reads books and writes "long papers on the twins in James Joyce" (*B,* 148) and is dreadfully afraid of marriage; Elly, who is no student, dreams of marrying a "virile but tender garage mechanic and hav[ing] a big cowy family" (*B,* 149). Esther feels smothered by the expectations of family and friends; Elly is an orphan.

It is appropriate for Elly to have neither family nor roots, for she represents escape from all of the pressures that are the source of Esther's confusion. In so doing, Elly brings that confusion into sharper relief. Esther is an unwilling captive of her background and conditioning; external familial and social pressures war with her natural instincts, and her level of self-confidence is far too low for those instincts to assert themselves sufficiently. Her naive expectations of sex and marriage, for example, have been thoroughly conditioned by her mother and by others: to be acceptable as a wife she must remain a virgin, and after marriage she must assume a submissive domestic role. Instinctively she rebels against these notions, partly because she naturally senses their limitations, and partly because she discovers that men are not bound by similar premarital rules. The confusion thereby produced is extreme. For

19-year-old Esther, "pureness [is] the great issue" (B, 90). Because she does not want "infinite security and to be the place an arrow shoots off from" (B, 92), as advocated by Buddy Willard and his mother, she decides that she must never marry. And because she now sees "the world divided into people who had slept with somebody and people who hadn't," she resolves to cross "the boundary line" (B, 90). Yet her conditioning remains a powerful influence; she can be comfortable with neither alternative.

Indeed, Esther finds it impossible to pursue either alternative in even a remotely satisfying way. "I wondered," she muses, "why I couldn't go the whole way doing what I should any more. This made me sad and tired. Then I wondered why I couldn't go the whole way doing what I shouldn't, . . . and this made me even sadder and more tired" (B, 32). It is the tiredness of depression that Esther feels, a depression produced by the immobility that baffles and frustrates her. Esther is indeed trapped within the stifling confines of the bell jar.

Unable to establish and nurture a self-identity that will afford her some measure of security, Esther is reduced to deriving her identity from the expectations of others. She acts. For Doreen, she must be worldly and blasé; for Buddy Willard, she must be pure and virginal; for Jay Cee, she must be intelligent and ambitious; for Mrs. Willard, she must be domestic and submissive; for her mother, she must be the good daughter, appropriately grateful, successful, and innocent. And above all, she must maintain at any cost a proper appearance of health and sanity, not, as her mother puts it, "like that," like "those awful dead people at that hospital" (B, 163). The more Esther acts in these ways, the more she loses touch with her self. The result is further loss of confidence and growing disorientation.

Another result of her role-playing is that Esther feels placed in a defensive position, for in responding to the expectations of others, she allows herself to be acted upon. She comes, therefore, to see her environment as increasingly hostile and threatening. Things accost her. On a skiing trip with Buddy, the rope tow is a "rough, bruising snake of a rope that slithered through [her fingers]" (B, 106). People menace her. Esther is terrified by the "brown figure in sensible flat brown shoes" (B, 150) whose appearance on the Boston Common abruptly ends her conversation with the sailor; in the presence of this ominous Mrs. Willard—Mrs. Greenwood person, Esther feels stricken with fear and guilt about her present behavior. She also experiences a sudden, sharp insight: "I thought what an awful woman that lady in the brown suit had been, and how she . . . was responsible for my taking the wrong turn here and the wrong path there and for everything bad that happened after that" (*B*, 151). Men especially threaten her; the reality of them always fails her expectation. The woman-hating Marco actually attacks her. From her experience with Buddy Willard, she knows that as "flawless" as men may seem "off in the distance," they would not "do at all" when they "moved closer" (*B*, 92). Marriage, then, is impossible for Esther since she knows that any man, even the handsome Constantin, would require that his wife become a domestic drudge, like Mrs. Willard's kitchen mat. Sex terrifies her; Esther's description of Buddy's penis is particularly devastating and dehumanizing: "The only thing I could think of was turkey neck and turkey gizzards" (*B*, 75).

The novel's Rosenberg motif illuminates that frame of mind. The summer Esther Greenwood goes to New York is also, as *The Bell Jar*'s opening lines reveal, "the summer they electrocuted the Rosenbergs" (*B*, 1). Esther observes: "It had nothing to do with me, but I couldn't help wondering what it would be like, being burned alive all along your nerves" (*B*, 1). Despite the disclaimer, the Rosenbergs' experience comes to have a great deal to do with Esther. By the time she becomes Dr. Gordon's patient, her confusion is far advanced; virtually incapable of action, she has become the helpless object of the acts of others. The clumsily applied shock treatment represents the epitome of such acts, and, significantly, it comes to serve as the symbol of Esther's paranoia and the total collapse of her perspective. The Rosenbergs, possibly innocent but helpless before the judgment of their accusers, have been put to death by electrocution. Esther instinctively equates their experience with her own; like the Rosenbergs, she feels powerless and victimized, threatened and judged by everyone and everything. Thus, as her own experience with electric shock commences, Esther wonders "what terrible thing it was that I had done" (*B*, 161).

## The Bell Jar

Placed in such a precarious emotional position by her insecurity and disorientation, the embattled Esther finds it more and more difficult to connect inner with outer reality. She is caught in a vicious round of destructive activity, for as her behavior has indicated, her very efforts at coping with her world also reinforce her isolation. Her voice expresses the dilemma. Esther's tone, especially up to the time of her recovery under Dr. Nolan's guidance, is similar to the tone of such late poems as

"Lady Lazarus" and "The Applicant": carefully postured, mocking, caus-
tic, defensively nonchalant. It is the voice that Esther feels encouraged
by Doreen's influence to develop: "wise and cynical as all hell" (B, 9).
Esther's wit is brilliant, and her humorous observations are incisive.
Such a voice can protect, but it can also protect too well, building an
impregnable barrier between its speaker and the world, between the self
and other people.

The condition is realized in the novel's dominant image; Esther feels
as though she is "being stuffed farther and farther into a black, airless
sack with no way out" (B, 144). She is increasingly unable to deal with
her environment, progressively helpless to "steer anything, not even
myself," powerless to "get myself to react" (B, 3). The glass walls of the
bell jar permit only a tantalizing, often distorted visual contact between
inside and outside; all other forms of mutual communication are impossible. And the interior environment not only isolates; it stifles. Esther
observes: "The air of the bell jar wadded round me and I couldn't stir"
(B, 210). Total withdrawal becomes Esther's only course of action. "To
the person in the bell jar . . . the world itself is the bad dream" (B, 267),
she concludes, and escape from that dream with its impossible demands
and pressures can be achieved only by return to an earlier, simpler time.
"I was only purely happy," she observes, "until I was nine years old"
(B, 82): what she seeks, then, is the singleness, the simplicity, and the
purity of infancy.

The actions Esther takes to achieve this end involve a kind of ritual
purgation, a means by which she can free herself of uncleanliness or confusion or guilt. To restore herself to a state of simple purity, she must
destroy or dissolve all evidence of the "bad dream." Plath also employs
that kind of action in the imagery of many of her last poems; release
from the oppression of the speaker's present condition is often expressed
in terms of death, purification, and rebirth. Similarly, Esther Greenwood, having returned from an evening of being Elly with Doreen and
Lenny, seeks to rid herself of the whole dirty, oppressive experience
through the rebirth of a sort of baptism:

> I said to myself: "Doreen is dissolving, Lenny Shepherd is dissolving,
> Frankie is dissolving, New York is dissolving, they are all dissolving away
> and none of them matter any more. I don't know them, I have never
> known them and I am very pure. All that liquor and those sticky kisses I
> saw and the dirt that settled on my skin on the way back is turning to
> something pure."

> The longer I lay there in the clear hot water the purer I felt, and when
> I stepped out at last and wrapped myself in one of the big, soft white
> hotel bath towels I felt pure and sweet as a new baby. (*B*, 22)

The bath, in this case, achieves the required retrogression, restoring
Esther's spirit without doing violence to her body. As her sense of
oppression intensifies, however, so does her need for escape, rendering
her ever more careless of physical consequences. Buddy Willard's pro-
posal of marriage places Esther in a particularly critical position, especially because her refusal expresses a rebellion she is not equipped to
handle. Skiing with Buddy shortly thereafter, then, she again seeks to
rid herself of her present world with its intolerable pressures and
demands; this time her need is so great that even the death of her physical body is unimportant: "The thought that I might kill myself formed
in my mind coolly as a tree or a flower" (*B*, 107). An inexperienced
skier, she takes off down the hill: "I thought, 'this is what it is to be
happy.' I plummeted down past the zigzaggers, the students, the
experts, through year after year of doubleness and smiles and compromise, into my own past. People and trees receded on either hand like the
dark sides of a tunnel as I hurtled on to the still, bright point at the end
of it, the pebble at the bottom of the well, the white sweet baby cradled
in its mother's belly" (*B*, 108).

From there, it is only a small step to Esther's actual suicide attempt,
for that act represents for her a total withdrawal to the "pure" and
"sweet" condition of infancy. The location she chooses is a dark hole
beneath her house, a "secret, earth-bottomed crevice" leading from the
cellar, lit only by "a dim, undersea light." After some effort, Esther
crawls into the hole, "crouch[ing] at the mouth of the darkness," and
covers the entrance with a log. The earth inside her womb-like retreat is
"friendly"; the dark feels "thick as velvet"; the cobwebs are soft; she
curls up and takes her sleeping pills (*B*, 190–91).

## Recovery and Prognosis

From this experience, Esther does achieve a sort of rebirth, though perhaps not precisely the variety she had expected. Her suicide attempt
fails, and she is hospitalized. Yet, in her total collapse, she has reached a
kind of infancy from which she can grow. Depressed beyond the point of
caring about "the doubleness and smiles and compromise," and encouraged by the sensitive Dr. Nolan to rediscover herself on her own terms,

Esther slowly constructs for herself a new and better-integrated personality.

She learns to free herself from the tyranny of others' expectations. Helpless to act even defensively during the days immediately following her suicide attempt, she has no choice but to appear exactly as she is. Her legs may look "disgusting and ugly" when Buddy Willard comes to visit, but she makes no move to hide them." " 'That's me,' " she thinks. " 'That's what I am' " (B, 195). When a group of medical students passing her bed greets her with the customary "How are you feeling?" she responds not with the expected "Fine" but with a truthful "I feel lousy" (B, 200). Once she is able to reveal her true self in this rudimentary way, Esther develops new confidence and perspective. In the presence of her hospital visitors, she identifies the tyranny that has held her captive, and she grows to hate these visits because she knows that the visitors measure her "fat and stringy hair against what I had been and what they wanted me to be" (B, 228). She then sees that such an attitude has motivated even the apparently beneficent interest of people like Jay Cee and the famous career-oriented woman poet at her college: "they all wanted to adopt me in some way, and, for the price of their care and influence, have me resemble them" (B, 248). Slowly Esther grows to understand the futility of building her identity on the expectations of people like these.

Perhaps the visitor most threatening to Esther's new perspective is her mother. Of all the forces that have kept Esther divided against herself, her mother has been the most powerful, looming up as the "brown figure" did that day on the Boston Common to assert her influence. Pious self-abnegation has been one of the mother's tools, and she attempts to use it still; during one of her visits, "my mother told me I should be grateful. She said I had used up almost all her money" (B, 209). Guilt keeps the daughter under control, and Esther, although seeing herself manipulated in this way, nevertheless feels the bell jar descending around her once again. On other occasions, however, Esther challenges her mother's influence more successfully. Of all her visitors, Esther observes, "my mother was the worst. She never scolded me, but kept begging me, with a sorrowful face, to tell her what she had done wrong" (B, 228). Following one of these sessions she dares to reveal to Dr. Nolan that she hates her mother—and then waits "for the blow to fall." Marvelously, however, Dr. Nolan replies only that " 'I suppose you do' " (B, 229). With such support, Esther grows able to accept and deal with her rebellion. She recalls a recent visit from her mother, whose face had been "a pale, reproachful moon." "A daughter in an asylum! I had done that to her" had been the mother's implied message. And "with her sweet, martyr's smile," she had said: " 'We'll take up where we left off, Esther. . . . We'll act as if this were a bad dream' " (B, 267). But Esther knows that she must do nothing of the kind.

Indeed, Esther achieves sufficient perspective to see that her struggle against the tyranny of custom and expectation is not hers alone but is characteristic of the human condition. Her hospital environment is little different from the college environment she has left and to which she will return. Like her and her hospital friends, her college friends, "too, sat under bell jars of a sort" (B, 268). Further, her new perspective allows her to deal with the "bad dream" from which her mother wishes her to seek escape. "Remember[ing] everything," she can now shun the idea that "forgetfulness, like a kind of snow, should numb and cover" the particulars of that nightmare. For "they were part of me. They were my landscape" (B, 267). The bell jar has been raised; it now hangs, "suspended, a few feet above my head. I was open to the circulating air" (B, 242).

Several other events herald Esther's emergence from the stifling confines of the bell jar. For the first time since the opening of her narrative, she laughs. In a conversation with Buddy Willard concerning the suicide of their friend Joan, Esther, confident in her own evaluation of the situation and accurate in her assessment of Buddy's confusion, "burst out laughing" (B, 270). To be sure, Esther's observations throughout the course of her narrative have not been without humor, but this laugh is different. This is not, like the others, an inward-directed, self-conscious quip or a sardonic gibe; it is the outward-directed, spontaneous response of a person secure enough to have no need of sarcasm. And that laugh, as it signals Esther's new freedom from the tyranny of her old self, provides a new perspective for the reader as well; the barriers between Esther and the world are removed not only for Esther, but also for her audience.

Joan's death affords Esther another opportunity to exercise her new perspective. During the conversation in which Esther laughs, Buddy is concerned that he, somehow, is responsible for the suicide attempts of Joan and Esther, both of whom he had dated. Esther, having already overcome, with Dr. Nolan's help, the fear of her own culpability, assumes the role of healer as she allays Buddy's apprehensions. Even more important for Esther, however, is the symbolic significance of Joan's death. "I wondered," she muses at Joan's funeral, "what I thought I was burying" (*B*, 273). Like the old Esther, Joan had been tyrannized by the brown Boston Common mother figure, yet Joan had been unable to identify the source of her oppression. Unlike Esther, Joan had been eager for Buddy to bring his mother to visit at the hospital. Thus, Esther knows that Joan is a reminder "of what I had been, and what I had been through" (*B*, 246). Joan's burial, then, signifies an aspect of Esther's new freedom, for what Esther buries at Joan's funeral is a part of her old, captive self.

Another symbol of Esther's new freedom is her diaphragm. As she points out, its acquisition frees her from the fear of unwanted pregnancy with its several undesirable consequences. She is no longer a sexual victim; even though her fear of marriage persists, she may now control her own fate. And the liberation afforded by this new control permits Esther to come to terms with her sexual identity. Able at last to put aside the blandishments of her mother and Mrs. Willard, Esther is free to shed the virginity that has been such an intolerable psychological burden to her old self. She thus is able to resolve the ambivalence that has so destructively divided her; the division of character represented by the former, oppressed Esther and her wish-fulfilling Elly Higginbottom is no longer necessary. Significantly, as Esther narrates the particulars of her tryst with Irwin, on whom she practices her "new, normal personality" (*B*, 254), she fails to mention the name by which Irwin calls her. Surely she is no longer Elly, even though the experience is a sexual one. In leaving her narrator nameless, Plath represents the narrator's new wholeness, for she is no longer the old Esther, either. She is truly, as she observes, "my own woman" (*B*, 251).

Thus renewed, Esther awaits her expected dismissal from the hospital. She has been, as she puts it, "born twice—patched, retreaded and approved for the road" (*B*, 275). Her prognosis seems good; the "new, normal personality" with which she will meet the world may well be sufficiently strong to resist future breakdown. Indeed, at the time when she actually tells this story, Esther is someone's wife and the mother of a baby; she is, she says, "all right" (*B*, 4), and she uses some of the free gifts from her chaotic summer in New York as toys for her child. There is, however, also a note of warning sounded at the novel's close. A retreaded tire, surely, can come apart more readily than a new one. Further, Esther the narrator-character asks: "How did I know that someday—at college, in Europe, somewhere, anywhere—the bell jar, with its stifling distortions, wouldn't descend again?" (*B*, 271). No doubt this question offers further corroboration of Esther's new, realistic self so that the reader may safely assume that Esther's recovery is complete.

For in judging the ending of this novel, we must respect its fictional envelope and assess Esther's recovery by the criteria Plath establishes within the work. At the novel's close, Esther the narrator appears to be functioning well within a world of marriage and children; her description and analysis of Esther the character seems centered and discerning. *The Bell Jar* achieves its own fictive conclusion, which is far different from the conclusion its author eventually reaches. For Esther's autobiographical creator, the prognosis is dark indeed. Like the adult Esther who is recreating this narrative, Sylvia Plath is married and a mother. She is also "in Europe" (no mere coincidence that Esther the narrator-character should include such reference in her comment); she has suffered ill health, and her marriage is troubled. And, as we now know, for Sylvia Plath the bell jar did "descend again." Only months after the novel was accepted for publication, its author attempted suicide for the second and final time.

## *Johnny Panic and the Bible of Dreams*

First published in Britain in 1977, *Johnny Panic and the Bible of Dreams* is a collection of Plath's short stories, related journal entries, and essays.[1] As Ted Hughes states in his 1978 introduction to the 1979 Harper and Row edition of the book, "This present collection contains the thirteen stories published in [the] 1977 English edition, with a further seven selected from the Indiana archive" at the Indiana University's Lilly Library (*JP*, 7). All but one of the 20 stories are previously published in journals and magazines; all but one of the five journal entries are previously unpublished; and one of the five essays appears here for the first time. The collection is arranged by date of composition in reverse chronological order, from 1962 to the early 1950s.

Hughes's principle of selection seems guided by the relevance of these pieces of fiction and nonfiction to Plath's work as a poet, particularly as they illuminate the development of her image making and her voice. Hughes opens his introduction by telling us that "about seventy stories, mostly unpublished, are extant" (*JP*, 1); for this collection, he has chosen those that "seem interesting enough to keep" (*JP*, 7). (The only previously published story not included here is "And Summer Will Not Come Again," which appeared in *Seventeen* in 1950.) The 20 stories

that are included are, says Hughes, "all autobiography," and "all are cir-
cling the flames which the poetry, encouraged by 'Johnny Panic' and *The
Bell Jar*, eventually jumped into" ( *JP*, 5). The journal entries are character studies, exercises for fictional character development; Hughes's editorial decisions anticipate his choices for *The Journals of Sylvia Plath* four
years later, as he maintains the privacy of living individuals or holds
back "very private" material ( *JP*, 7). The essays, or the "bits of prose" as
Hughes calls them, come mostly from the time of *Ariel* and include the
twice-published "Ocean 1212-W" and the once-published and often-
quoted "Context." The other three essays are "America! America!" and
"A Comparison" (also previously published) and "Snow Blitz," a 1963
essay recounting (almost cheerfully) Plath's winter difficulties in her
London flat.

In the excellent reviews of *Johnny Panic*, commentary mostly follows
Hughes's theme, the reviewers finding the volume's main value in the
contents' illumination of Plath's poetry. Emily Leider concludes, for
example, that "the prose in *Panic* should be read along with *Letters Home*
and *The Bell Jar* as background for the poems, to help fill the gaps in our
understanding of an awesome mind, talent, vision."[2] Margaret Atwood,
dubbing the volume a "prose catch-all" and noting that even the "fairly
dismal stories" are "revealing," calls attention to their "insights into
[Plath's] own emotional mainsprings that characterize her poetry."[3]
Suzanne Juhasz observes that "one can see these pieces as important in a
negative way, examples of Plath short-circuiting her own genius in her
unceasing bid for acceptance."[4] Katha Pollitt finds in *Johnny Panic*'s
prose evidence of Plath's ambivalence, apparent elsewhere, about "her
capacity to lead what she saw as a normal life, involving men, houses,
and babies and solid, permanent connections to other people."[5]

## The Stories: Ritual and Ambivalence

Pollitt points toward a notable motif of this collection, particularly evident in the stories, of ritual and ambivalence. In "Sunday at the
Mintons'," Plath's narrative voice comments that Elizabeth "winced
under the benevolent brightness of Henry's patronizing smile. She
wanted to say something brave and impudent, then, something that
would disturb the awful serenity of his features" ( *JP*, 301). The disturbance of "awful serenity" is a subtext in many of these stories, a "serenity" that is "awful" because of its thoughtless conventionality and casual
disregard of individual human necessity. Much of this fiction explores

the positive values of perseverance, spontaneity, and connectedness with the inner self, often played out against shallow and rigid custom.

The story "The Fifty-ninth Bear" enacts "a ritual of penance and forgiveness" where the principal characters, Sadie and Norton, reflect and extend the dynamics of Elizabeth and Henry in "Sunday at the Mintons'." In "The Daughters of Blossom Street" and "Johnny Panic and the Bible of Dreams," apparent subversion of Christian ritual and dogma appears finally as Plath's own peculiar and passionate affirmation. The character Billy in "Daughters" is a man of both limited mental ability and spontaneous action who dies helping others: "He wouldn't of [*sic*] died," observes one character, "if he hadn't been helping out other folks." In "Johnny Panic," the title character is a king of dreams and a high priest of madness who wages battle with doctors and psychiatrists, the "false priests" of normalcy. The story's apocalyptic close involves sacrifice, death, and resurrection.

"Mothers," the only story in *Johnny Panic* from the year before Plath's death, deserves a closer look. Esther, the story's main character, has recently moved to a manor farm in Devon with her family—her husband, Tom (a writer), and their baby daughter. Pregnant with their second child and hoping to become better acquainted with her neighbors, Esther has accepted the invitation of her neighbor Rose to attend a meeting of the town's "Mothers' Union" at the local church. With Esther and Rose on this November day is another neighbor, Mrs. Nolan, the wife of the local pub-keeper, who also knows only a few people in the town even though she has lived there for six years. She feels very much the outsider, and as the story progresses it is clear that she will maintain her distance, as indicated, in one way, by the narrator's never telling us Mrs. Nolan's first name (at the same time that we are not told Esther's or Rose's last name).

Complicating these neighborly dynamics is the church itself and Esther's physical and spiritual relation to it. The church is gloomy and menacing; its floor gives off a "deadly" and "primeval cold" ( *JP*, 15); the rector is a forbidding "black figure" wearing a "black hat" ( *JP*, 14). (By contrast, the front door of Esther's house is "yellow-painted and flanked by two pungent bushes of box" [ *JP*, 10], and Esther is sewing a yellow flannel nightdress for her baby.) Yet Esther feels drawn by the church carillon, with its "probing notes" ( *JP*, 13). She was raised a Unitarian but suspects that she is an atheist; she is keenly aware of "the vast, irrevocable gap between her faithless state and the beatitude of belief, yet "she [hasn't] the heart to tell the rector she had been through all this pious trying ten years before, in Comparative Religion classes at college, and only ended up sorry she was not a Jew" ( *JP*, 14). (Thus, perhaps, one reason for the use of the name "Esther," which Plath chooses for her character here and in *The Bell Jar*.)

Following the Mothers' Union meeting and church service, Esther, Rose, and Mrs. Nolan join the other women in the church hall, sharing a Eucharist-like repast of cakes and tea. Mrs. Nolan is "desperate" to find some common ground for conversation but speaks only with Esther. And because Mrs. Nolan is divorced, Esther learns, she will not be invited to join the Mothers' Union. Strangely, however, Mrs. Nolan is also described by the story's narrator as an "unhappy seeress," and as such, she seems meant to represent a very palpable aspect of Esther's character. As Rose's friend, Esther may be welcomed into the community, but her membership will be qualified and incomplete, a part of her glad to remain with Mrs. Nolan (echoing *The Bell Jar*'s Dr. Nolan), the outsider.

This ambivalence of character, reflecting conflicting and probably incompatible identities, is one we see elsewhere in Plath. Like Esther in "Mothers," the protagonist of *The Bell Jar*, also named Esther, has two friends. Betsy (like Rose in "Mothers") personifies Esther's domestic and obedient tendencies, valuing domesticity, wifehood, motherhood, sewing skills, gardening, and conventionality. Doreen, on the other hand (like Mrs. Nolan in "Mothers"), encourages and reflects Esther's rebellious and iconoclastic side. But "Mothers" carries this duality a step further than *The Bell Jar*, for in "Mothers" the ambivalence is also internalized; Esther needs no Elly Higginbottom to personify her instinctive, unpatterned self.

As Ted Hughes and many others point out, these stories are autobiographical. In them, Plath not only investigates problematic life circumstances (marriage, motherhood, community, individuality) but also explores and objectifies contentious facets of her inner landscape (her feelings about marriage, motherhood, community, and individuality). The stories, together with the essays and journal entries, thereby provide another tool for illuminating the attitudes and feelings of the poet. We find in these stories, as in Plath's poetry, ambivalence, anger, and sometimes joy regarding both Plath's psyche and the constellation of characters surrounding her. As in "Mothers," we see a ritual of belonging vainly imposed upon the iconoclastic self, which promises to break free of the black rector and of "Tom."

# Chapter Five
# Early Poetry

For the purpose of discussing and analyzing Plath's poetry, we can profitably observe the chronological grouping in which the poems naturally and appropriately arrange themselves. The work of any poet, of course, reveals both subtle and significant change as it progresses from early to late, from experimentation to maturity; Sylvia Plath's work is no exception. Her poetry, however, lends itself especially well to close chronological scrutiny, for her thematic concerns remain relatively constant throughout; Ted Hughes, Plath's poet husband, reminds us "how faithfully her separate poems build up into one long poem."[1] The principal changes in Plath's poetry are technical and structural, moving from the experimental quality of the early group through the transitional quality of the middle group to the mastery of the late. The reader who seeks full understanding of Plath's excellent late poems is well advised to examine first the earlier foundation upon which that work is built.

Plath's early poetry is collected principally in *The Colossus*; of her four published volumes, this is the only one that appeared during her lifetime. The contents of the British edition of this volume (published in 1960 as *The Colossus and Other Poems*) and the American edition (published in 1962) differ slightly; 10 of the poems in the English volumes do not appear in the American. These poems—"Black Rook in Rainy Weather," "The Beast," "Dark House," "Maenad," "Maudlin," "Who," "Metaphors," "Ouija," "Two Sisters of Persephone," and "Witch Burning"—are included, instead, in the later American volume *Crossing the Water* (1971). Nevertheless, these poems do belong to Sylvia Plath's early period and should be considered as such. They, with the other *Colossus* poems, were written between 1955, when Plath first went to Cambridge as a Fulbright scholar, and 1959, when she toured the United States in preparation for her permanent return to England.

Ted Hughes's helpful notes in "The Chronological Order of Sylvia Plath's Poems" and in his introduction to *The Collected Poems*[2] permit us specifically to date the composition of most of these *Colossus* poems (even though the information in these two pieces sometimes conflicts). One group was written between early 1956 and 1957, during Plath's two years at Cambridge. Specifically, "Faun," "Strumpet Song," "Spinster," "All the Dead Dears," "Two Sisters of Persephone," "Maudlin," "Black Rook in Rainy Weather," and "Watercolor of Grantchester Meadows" belong to Plath's years at Cambridge; "Departure" was written in Benidorm, Spain, during the summer following Plath's marriage to Hughes; and "Hardcastle Crags" and "Sow" were inspired by Plath's visit to the home of Hughes's parents in West Yorkshire. A second group was written during 1957–1958, the year of Plath's return from England to teach English at Smith College. "Ouija" was written in 1957, and a visit to Cape Cod in the summer of 1957 produced "Mussel Hunter at Rock Harbor." "The Thin People," "Lorelei," "Full Fathom Five," "Frog Autumn," "The Disquieting Muses," "Snakecharmer," "The Ghost's Leavetaking," "Sculptor," and "Night Shift" were written during the following year in Northampton, Massachusetts, and "Moonrise," "The Companionable Ills," "I Want, I Want," and "The Times Are Tidy" were also written in 1958. A third group of poems belong to 1958–1959, when Plath and Hughes lived on Boston's Beacon Hill; these are "The Eye-Mote," "The Man in Black," "The Hermit at Outermost House," "The Beekeeper's Daughter," "Point Shirley," "Aftermath," "Two Views of a Cadaver Room," and "Suicide off Egg Rock." Also written in 1959 were "The Bull of Bendylaw," "Medallion," and "The Colossus." Finally, "Blue Moles," "The Winter Ship," "Mushrooms," "The Burnt-out Spa," "The Manor Garden," and the "Poem for a Birthday" sequence ("Who," "Dark House," "Maenad," "The Beast," "Flute Notes from a Reedy Pond," "Witch Burning," and "The Stones") were written during the fall of 1959 at Yaddo, following Plath's summer trip across the United States and just before her return to England. "Metaphors," written in 1959, was first published in 1960 as "Metaphors for a Pregnant Woman."

Of course, there are among the poems of Sylvia Plath's early period a number that she chose not to include in *The Colossus*. She wrote poetry from a very early age, and she composed the first *Colossus* poems when she was 24. There are many poems, then, that belong to the fairly substantial pre-*Colossus* period, and there are, as well, several poems written between 1955 and 1959 but not collected in the early volume. Because some of those now appear in *The Collected Poems* in the sections entitled "Juvenalia" and "Poems 1956–1963," and since several are also collected and dated in two limited-edition volumes, *Crystal Gazer* and *Lyonnesse*, published in 1971 by London's Rainbow Press, it is possible to date the early, non-*Colossus* poems that will be discussed in this chapter. These are "Admonitions" and "Dream of the Hearse-Driver," written in 1950–1951; "Mad Girl's Love Song," written in 1951; "Circus in Three Rings" and "Lament," written in 1951–1952; "Metamorphoses of the Moon," written in 1953; "Crystal Gazer," "Tinker Jack and the Tidy Wives," and "Wreath for a Bridal," written in 1956; "The Other Two," written in 1957; and "A Winter's Tale," written in 1958. Finally, Plath's own commentary about her work, included in *Letters Home*, permits us to date the composition of three other non-*Colossus* poems with which this chapter shall deal. These poems, written during Plath's undergraduate days at Smith College, are "To Eva Descending the Stair" (1954), "Doomsday" (1954), and "Temper of Time" (1955).

Plath's early poetry is both technically and thematically significant, for scattered through the early poems are most of the elements that later fuse into the final, powerful outbursts of the mature poetry. We find in this early work the sense of doom and the fascination with disintegration and death so central to the later poems. We see as well the ambivalence toward sex, wifehood, and motherhood. The propensity to nightmare is here, too, as are many initial uses of the later, more skillfully handled set of images.

When viewed as part of her entire canon, Plath's early poetry displays a certain experimental quality. In contrast with the spontaneous, raw force of her late work, Plath's early poems seem generally contrived, mannered, and self-conscious, features apparently caused by her tendency to create artificial divisions in the essentially single dilemma she faces in these poems and by her reluctance to confront directly various difficult subjects. In the sense that the poet's perceptions in these works appear generally less well informed than they do in the later poems, the poetry suffers from too little control; and in the sense that content sometimes seems artificially manipulated to fit a set structure, they suffer from too much.

## Doom and Resistance: A Precarious Balance

Much of the early poetry is death-directed. The sense of impending doom is often couched in somber terms, and death waits in a diffuse gothic landscape:

> An ill wind is stalking
> while evil stars whir

> and all the gold apples
> go bad to the core.
>
> . . . . . . . . . . . . . . . . . .
> Through closets of copses
> tall skeletons walk
> while nightshade and nettles
> tangle the track.
>
> . . . . . . . . . . . . . . . . . .
> His wife and his children
> hand riddled with shot,
> there's a hex on the cradle
> and death in the pot.[3]

Yet, as in this poem, the gothicism seems frequently imposed for effect rather than included by necessity. Thus, in much of Plath's early work, the vague sense of doom is not always given an origin; rather, nature is presented as menacing, as antipathetic to the speaker in a general, undefined way:

> The figs on the fig tree in the yard are green;
> Green, also, the grapes on the green vine
> Shading the brickred porch tiles.
> The money's run out.
>
> How nature, sensing this, compounds her bitters.
> Ungifted, ungrieved, our leavetaking.
> . . . . . . . . . . . . . . . . . . . . . . . . . . . . . . . . . . . . .
> The scraggy rock spit shielding the town's blue bay
> Against which the brunt of outer sea
> Beats, is brutal endlessly.[4]

If we use other available information as a gloss, however, some of the poetic references may yield more meaning and perhaps more power. In *The Bell Jar*, Esther Greenwood is profoundly affected by a story of a fig tree. She later imagines each fig to represent a direction her life might take: "I saw my life branching out before me like the green fig tree in the story," and yet she feels powerless to act or to choose: "I saw myself sitting in the crotch of this fig tree, starving to death, just because I couldn't make up my mind which of the figs I would choose. I wanted each and every one of them, but choosing one meant losing all the rest, and, as I sat there, unable to decide, the figs began to wrinkle and go black, and, one by one, they plopped to the ground at my feet" (*B*, 84, 85).

Still, in many of the early poems, the poet's attitude toward the inevitability of death is ambivalent, revealing sometimes resignation, sometimes fear, sometimes regret, and sometimes decided resistance. Though she can state that "The money's run out," or that there's "death in the pot," the poems do not quite convince us that she really means it.

In fact, this very unconvincing quality of some of the early poems reveals a tendency that distinguishes them from the late. In a few of the early works, Plath expresses a number of positive, optimistic attitudes quite absent from her later poetry. For example, the very early villanelle "Lament" is the poet's lament for the death of her father. Although the father is represented in this poem as the imposing, colossal figure of such later (but still "early") poems as "The Colossus," "Man in Black," and "The Beekeeper's Daughter," he is not awarded the threatening, tyrannical posture of those poems. The poet's implicit attitude in "Lament" is one not of dread, but of admiration:

> The sting of bees took away my father
> Who walked in a swarming shroud of wings
> And scorned the tick of the falling weather.
>
> . . . . . . . . . . . . . . . . . . . . . . . . . . . . . .
>
> Trouncing the sea like a raging bather,
> He rode the flood in a pride of prongs
> And scorned the tick of the falling weather.
>
> . . . . . . . . . . . . . . . . . . . . . . . . . . . . . .
>
> O ransack the four winds and find another
> Man who can mangle the grin of kings:
> The sting of bees took away my father
> Who scorned the tick of the falling weather.[5]

Similarly, and relatedly, the poet's attitude toward marriage in some of the early poems is far more sanguine than in the later ones. In a poem composed at the commencement of her own marriage, Plath writes:

From this holy day on, all pollen blown
Shall strew broadcast so rare a seed on wind
That every breath, thus teeming, set the land
Sprouting fruit, flowers, children most fair in legion
To slay spawn of dragon's teeth: speaking this promise,
Let flesh be knit, and each step hence go famous.[6]

The fantastic puns in this poem seem to lend a slightly ironic edge to
the tone; still, the attitude remains one of hope and blessing. In other
poems, the threat suggested here by "spawn of dragon's teeth" figures
more heavily, yet the possibility of failure does not obliterate the belief
in success. In "The Other Two," for instance, though the married pair is
happy, they are dogged by their doom-doubles:

We dreamed their arguments, their stricken voices.
We might embrace, but those two never did,
Come, so unlike us, to a stiff impasse,
Burdened in such a way we seemed the lighter—
Ourselves the haunters and they, flesh and blood;
As if, above love's ruinage, we were
The heaven those two dreamed of, in despair.[7]

And in "Crystal Gazer," the gypsy who promises good fortune to the
newlyweds has herself been doomed in love, Faust-like, for her passion
"To govern more sight than given to a woman / By wits alone." She sees:

Each love blazing blind to its gutted end—
And, fixed in the crystal center, grinning fierce:
Earth's ever-green death's head.[8]

On other subjects as well, Plath creates in these early poems a balance between confident and cynical attitudes. The villanelle "Admonitions" states a cautionary theme similar to that of "Crystal Gazer," but
with broader application:

From here the moon seems smooth as angel-food,
from here you can't see spots upon the sun;

never try to know more than you should.

. . . . . . . . . . . . . . . . . . . . . . . . . . .. . . . . . .

For deadly secrets strike when understood
and lucky stars all exit on the run:
never try to knock on rotten wood,
never try to know more than you should.[9]

And, expanding on the moon example of "Admonitions," the poem "Metamorphoses of the Moon" strikes a similar theme:

The choice between the mica mystery
of moonlight or the pockmarked face we see
through the scrupulous telescope
is always to be made: innocence
is a fairy-tale; intelligence
hangs itself on its own rope.[10]

To be sure, optimism is not rampant in any of these poems, which seem to have a damned-if-you-do-and-damned-if-you-don't attitude. Still, there remains a hope that the damning is not inevitable. Further, it is noteworthy that in the very early poem "Metamorphoses of the Moon" (1953), the moon has not yet come to reflect the deathlight of even the later early poetry. Perhaps what we see here is indeed a kind of metamorphosis; the moonlight's imagistic role as the light of deception in this poem could well be the logical predecessor of its later, familiar role as the cold light of blankness and death.

In fact, the moon does assume that more familiar meaning in the early poem "Hardcastle Crags." Here, as in other early poems, the poet expresses quite simultaneously her anticipation of inevitable doom and her urge to resist that inevitability. The woman in "Hardcastle Crags," taking a night walk in that stony, flinty landscape, turns away from the black indifference that threatens her there:

. . . before the weight
Of stones and hills of stones could break
Her down to mere quartz grit in that stony light
She turned back.

This resistance, this self-preserving instinct, is a significant feature of the early poems. And even where the poet shuns positive resistance to death or disintegration, she maintains in a number of poems a perspective less evident in her final work. In "Lorelei," though the speaker finally cannot resist the sirens' song, she can recognize the madness and destructiveness of it:

> Sisters, your song
> Bears a burden too weighty
> For the whorled ear's listening
>
> . . . . . , . . . . . . . . . . . . . . . . .
>
> Deranging by harmony
> Beyond the mundane order,
> Your voices lay siege.

And in "Black Rook in Rainy Weather," the poet still desires, nearly expects, the mundane order to provide flashes of significance—epiphanies, perhaps—if not design:

> I only know that a rook
> Ordering its black feathers can so shine
> As to seize my senses, haul
> My eyelids up, and grant
>
> A brief respite from fear
> Of total neutrality.[11]

There appears in this early work, then, a tension between death's allure and the poet's instinctive resistance to it. Certainly, resistance is most often momentary and impulsive, the desire for it being in some way overpowered by the claims of doom. Still, the balance between the claims of life and death, of self-preservation and destruction, is more even in the early poems than in the later ones.

Nevertheless, the quality of menace is ubiquitous in the early work, and it emanates everywhere from a natural landscape that is by turns inhospitable or threatening. Nearly any aspect of nature can serve as the agent of doom; often, as in "Lorelei," "Suicide off Egg Rock," "Full Fathom Five," "Mussel Hunter at Rock Harbor," or "Man in Black," or as in "Point Shirley," the sea is death's agent:

Steadily the sea
Eats at Point Shirley. She died blessed,
And I come by
Bones, bones only, pawed and tossed,
A dog-faced sea.
The sun sinks under Boston, bloody red.
("Point Shirley")

But menace may lurk, as well, in a flinty landscape ("Hardcastle Crags"), a museum relic ("All the Dead Dears"), a pair of dead moles ("Blue Moles"), a season of the year ("Frog Autumn"), or even an aggressive crop of new mushrooms: "We shall by morning / Inherit the earth. / Our foot's in the door" ("Mushrooms").

It is less my intent, however, to specify the sources of menace and death in these early poems than simply to recognize that these qualities form a consistent, unremitting ground bass throughout the works. The threat does indeed emanate in part from the sea, from the land, or from some vague natural or inanimate source. But whatever the origin, menace and danger remain a constant preoccupation—danger to Plath not only from external sources, but from herself. "Suicide off Egg Rock" relates a man's successful suicide attempt:

Behind him the hotdogs split and drizzled
On the public grills, and the ochreous salt flats,
Gas tanks, factory stacks—that landscape
Of imperfections his bowels were part of—
Rippled and pulsed in the glassy updraught.
Sun struck the water like a damnation.
No pit of shadow to crawl into,
And his blood beating the old tattoo
I am, I am, I am.

Everything shrank in the sun's corrosive
Ray but Egg Rock on the blue wastage.
He heard when he walked into the water

The forgetful surf creaming on those ledges.

When we compare these lines with an episode in *The Bell Jar*, we may surmise that this particular danger is one to which the poet herself feels fatally drawn. Esther Greenwood relates the events of a day of swimming at the beach with her companions Cal, Jody, and Mark:

> A smoke seemed to be going up from my nerves like the smoke from the grills and the sun-saturated road. The whole landscape—beach and headland and sea and rock—quavered in front of my eyes like a stage backcloth. . . .
> I thought I would swim out until I was too tired to swim back. As I paddled on, my heartbeat boomed like a dull motor in my ears.
> I am I am I am. . . .
> I paddled my hands in the water and kicked my feet. The egg-shaped rock didn't seem to be any nearer than it had been when Cal and I had looked at it from the shore. . . .
> The only thing to do was to drown myself then and there. (*B*, 176–80)

A closer look at a few specific poems will afford a clearer understanding of not only the quality of menace but also the concrete, individual ways that quality is rendered. "The Manor Garden," for example, presents a kind of monologue in which the pregnant mother poignantly warns her baby that death and difficulty are conditions to which he is to be born. This work, which anticipates such later poems as "Morning Song," "You're," and "Balloons," is one of the best in *Colossus*; its metaphors are marvelously precise and its knitting of images affords a fine balance among the mother's feelings of love, regret, and dread:

> The fountains are dry and the roses over.
> Incense of death. Your day approaches.
> The pears fatten like little buddhas.
> A blue mist is dragging the lake.
>
> . . . . . . . . . . . . . . . . . . . . . . . . . . . . . .
>
> You inherit white heather, a bee's wing,
> Two suicides, the family wolves,
> Hours of blankness.
>
> . . . . . . . . . . . . . . . . . . . . . . . . . . . . . .
>
> The small birds converge, converge
> with their gifts to a difficult borning.

Another poem, "Two Views of a Cadaver Room," anticipates the later "Death & Co." with its two—predator and lover—faces of death. "Two Views," one of the finest poems in *Colossus*, describes in its first section a girl's visit to "the dissecting room":

> The day she visited the dissecting room
> They had four men laid out, black as burnt turkey,
> Already half unstrung. A vinegary fume
> Of the death vats clung to them;
> The white-smocked boys started working.
> The head of his cadaver had caved in,
> And she could scarcely make out anything
> In that rubble of skull plates and old leather.
> A sallow piece of string held it together.
>
> In their jars the snail-nosed babies moon and glow.
> He hands her the cut-out heart like a cracked heirloom.

and in its second section a Breughel painting:

> In Brueghel's panorama of smoke and slaughter
> Two people only are blind to the carrion army:
> . . . . . . . . . . . . . . . . . . . . . . . . . . . . . . .
> These Flemish lovers flourish; not for long.
>
> Yet desolation, stalled in paint, spares the little country
> Foolish, delicate, in the lower right-hand corner.

As M. L. Rosenthal observes, this whole poem reveals "some flashes of the long-standing imminence in Sylvia Plath of her final kind of aware-ness," especially in the "macabre" 10th line ("In their jars . . .") of the first section "with its grisly echo of Prufrock."[12] This image of death is one that deeply impresses Esther Greenwood in *The Bell Jar*, as well. In chapter 6, Esther describes an experience nearly identical with the first section of "Two Views," during a tour with Buddy Willard of a cadaver room in his medical school. And elsewhere, Esther comments: "I thought drowning must be the kindest way to die, and burning the worst. Some of those babies in the jars that Buddy Willard showed me had gills, he said" (*B*, 177).

Closely related to this figure is the image of death explored in "Medallion." If the speaker holds a "cut-out heart" in "Two Views of a Cadaver Room," in "Medallion" she holds a dead snake that glitters in the sun. The associations of death with glitter so numerous in the late poetry are obvious in this poem. And we see here as well an early expression of Plath's association of death with chastity and perfection (evident in such *Ariel* poems as "Edge," "Fever 103°," and "A Birthday Present"): "Knifelike, he was chaste enough, / Pure death's metal. The yardman's / Flung brick perfected his laugh."

A different kind of attitude toward death is presented in "To Eva Descending the Stair," a villanelle in which word order sometimes seems tampered with for the sake of rhyme. Here the menace comes not from tangible nature but from time, and the poet indicates that time, even though it may be destructive, has not yet stopped: "Clocks cry: stillness is a lie, my dear; / The wheels revolve, the universe keeps running. / Proud you halt upon the spiral stair."[13] But if "clocks cry" and "stillness," the condition of death in the later poetry, "is a lie" at one moment, time crashingly halts at another:

> Too late to ask if end was worth the means,
> Too late to calculate the toppling stock:
> The idiot bird leaps out and drunken leans.
> The hour is crowed in lunatic thirteens.[14]

Thematically, this poem points toward the final "too late" poems. And it is an early example of the hallucinatory, surreal quality of expression that becomes a salient characteristic of the poet's later work.

While Plath is experimenting in the early poems with the surrealist style she uses so effectively in the late work, she also explores the contents and materials of that mode. As surrealist art celebrates the mind's free operation and exploits, in part, the material of nightmare and dream and the mind's state between sleeping and waking, so Plath examines, in her early work, the actual content of dreams. In "The Dream of the Hearse-Driver," the driver himself describes his dreaming of the previous night:

"Last night," he said, "I slept well
except for two uncanny dreams
. . . . . . . . . . . . . . . . . . . . . . . .
"In the first dream I was driving
down the dark in a black hearse
with many men until I crashed
a light, and right away a raving
woman followed us and rushed
to halt our car in headlong course.
. . . . . . . . . . . . . . . . . . . . . . . .
"Behind me then I heard a voice
warning me to hold her hand
and kiss her on the mouth for she
loved me and a brave embrace
would avoid all penalty.
'I know, I know,' I told my friend.
. . . . . . . . . . . . . . . . . . . . . . . .
"I do not tell you the nightmare
which occurred to me in China."[15]

If Plath portrays the dream itself in "The Dream of the Hearse-Driver," she explores the time when dreams occur in "The Ghost's Leavetaking," the

chilly no-man's land of about
Five oclock in the morning, the no-colour void
Where the waking head rubbishes out the draggled lot
Of sulphurous dreamscapes and obscure lunar conundrums
Which seemed, when dreamed, to mean so profoundly much.

Both of these poems skillfully capture the quality of the dream and are highly successful in their exploration and evocation of the dream state. Furthermore, they indicate a direction Plath chose to abandon in her later poems—that of writing about the surrealist region of dream and nightmare, of the margin between waking and sleep, rather than of writing from that region.

Apparent in these early poems, then, are several features uncharacteristic of Plath's later work. Her emphasis on the sleeping, dreaming state as a region separate from the waking one is evident only in the early work; later, she adroitly, and terrifyingly, combines the two. And the whimsical and sometimes desperate optimism of some of the early poems becomes muted and changed in the later work.

Nevertheless, this optimism does not dominate even the early work, which is characterized generally by a wavering attitude toward time coupled with an abiding sense of doom. Sometimes, however, the brooding, gothic atmosphere and the general pronouncements of doom are replaced by a sort of wild defiance that, though surreal, goes far beyond the surrealism of "Doomsday" or "Temper of Time." In these poems, even though they may seem verbally stilted and structurally forced, one can detect the beginning of an energy bordering on hysteria that points directly to the later poems. It is useful to compare some of these madly energetic lines with an excerpt from a short autobiographical sketch of Sylvia Plath entitled "Ocean 1212-W" (1963), a sketch in which Plath recorded a number of impressions of the first nine years of her life on Cape Cod: "My final memory of the sea is of violence—a still, unhealthily yellow day in 1939, the sea molten, . . . heaving at its leash like a broody animal. . . . My brother and I . . . imbibed the talk of tidal waves . . . like a miracle elixir. This was a monstrous specialty, a leviathan. Our world might be eaten, blown to bits. We wanted to be on it. . . . The only sound was a howl, jazzed up by the bangs, slams, groans, and splintering of objects tossed like crockery in a giant's quarrel."[16]

> In the circus tent of a hurricane
> designed by a drunken god
> my extravagant heart blows up again
> in a rampage of champagne-colored rain
> and the fragments whir like a weather vane
> while the angels all applaud.
>                     ("Circus in Three Rings")[17]

Certainly, the comparison is instructive. Not only does it help to reinforce meanings already inherent in the poetry itself and to emphasize the intensely autobiographical nature of that poetry; it also points to the way external and internal landscape become inseparable in the later work. In the interpretation of the child's experience we can already hear the mocking, desperate tones of Lady Lazarus.

## Humor

This mocking, even occasionally humorous voice is, in fact, an aspect that should be stressed in discussing Plath's poetry. Certainly, although none of the poems is raucously funny, subtle humor is often present. And this is another feature that distinguishes the early work from the late; the humorous attitude of some of the early poems is one Plath seems to have relinquished by the time she wrote her final ones. In those, levity is diminished, and bitter mockery predominates.

The early poem "A Winter's Tale," for example, creates an amusing, almost funny, picture of the Boston Common at Christmas:

> By S. S. Pierce, by S. S. Pierce,
> The red-nosed, blue-nosed women ring
> For money. Lord, the crowds are fierce!
> There's carolling
>
> On Winter Street, on Temple Place.
> Poodles are baking cookies in
> Filene's show windows. Grant us grace,
> Donner, Blitzen.
>
> And all you Santa's deer who browse
> By leave of the Park Commission
> On grass that once fed Boston cows.[18]

Certainly the satiric tone so evident in many of Plath's later poems is here, but in this playful poem the satire is far less acrid.

In "Mushrooms," a wry, and even droll, kind of humor is achieved by rhythms:

> We are shelves, we are
> Tables, we are meek,
> We are edible,
>
> Nudgers and shovers
> In spite of ourselves.

by rhymes and word sounds:

> Overnight, very
> Whitely, discreetly,
> Very quietly,
>
> Our toes, our noses
> Take hold on the loam,
> Acquire the air.

And humor is achieved also by the very nature of the poem's speakers
and situation. Nor, as Israel Horovitz remarks, are the poem's "special
sly obscenities" to be overlooked.[19] Indeed, these obscenities together
with the wryness and subtlety of "Mushrooms" suggest the presence of a
feminist subtext. Although "we" mushrooms may grow in "loam,"
although we are "meek," we are "Nudgers and shovers / In spite of ourselves." And "We shall by morning / Inherit the earth. / Our foot's in the
door."

The playfulness of the riddle and the word game is again evoked in
"Metaphors," in which pregnancy is the answer to the riddle, and the
"nine syllables" indicate both the nine-syllable lines and the nine lines of
the poem as well as the nine months of pregnancy:

> I'm a riddle in nine syllables,
> An elephant, a ponderous house,
> A melon strolling on two tendrils.
> O red fruit, ivory, fine timbers!
> This loaf's big with its yeasty rising.
> Money's new-minted in this fat purse.
> I'm a means, a stage, a cow in calf.
> I've eaten a bag of green apples,
> Boarded the train there's no getting off.[20]

The train image here suggests none of the death-driven necessity of such
later, similar images as in "Getting There" and "Years." Yet, as it signifies birth and new life, the railroad image of "Metaphors" does point
toward the death-car of the late poems, anticipating the theme of birth-
death fusion so central to Plath's final vision.

Still another kind of humor, the black, sardonic humor achieved so effectively in the late poem "Lady Lazarus," is evident in the early work. We can recognize that mocking voice, which manages to ridicule both speaker and audience, not only in "Circus in Three Rings" but also in "Tinker Jack and the Tidy Wives":

> "Come lady, bring that pot
> Gone black of polish
> And whatever pan this mending master
> Should trim back to shape;
> I'll correct each mar
> On silver dish,
> And shine that kettle of copper
> Bright as blood."[21]

Thus, Plath's use of the comic mode in this early work reveals one direction that her poetry might have taken, and one that it did take. The jocularity evident in the early vision seems a quality that had little place in the late. To be sure, humor is not the major distinguishing feature of the early poems; in them, Plath's humor and pessimism seem almost to alternate between poems, with one or the other aspect governing a single work—and with the menacing, pessimistic attitude predominating. But in the darker vision of the late work, the humor gives way to the more bitter, satiric mode. There the poet employs her acerbic wit in a defensive way, using comedy to create a necessary distance between her painful subjects and her personal awareness of them. In *Ariel* and *Winter Trees*, the waggishness of "A Winter's Tale," the drollery of "Mushrooms," the playfulness of "Metaphors," and the mockery of "Tinker Jack and the Tidy Wives" fuse into a single kind of defiant, bitter comedy that is essential to the power not only of "Lady Lazarus" but also of many others.

## Conflict

Although Plath's pessimism in these early poems is not often assigned any specific cause, possible causes are suggested in the form of deeply rooted and potentially disabling emotional conflicts. We learn that she perceives her father to be rigid, stern, and black. Yet it is even more revealing that in all of "Ocean 1212-W," in which Plath provides considerable insight into the character of her grandparents, her mother, her brother, and even her uncle, the sole mention of her father appears in the closing words: "And this is how it stiffens, my vision of that seaside childhood. My father died, we moved inland."[22]

If there is scanty description of father, however, there is a wealth of suggestion regarding his effect on the poet's life. As seen in the passages quoted previously, she feels that his stifling rule has turned her to stone. "The Colossus," title poem of her first volume, is concerned on the literal level with a broken ancient statue: "I shall never get you put together entirely, / Pieced, glued, and properly jointed." Reference here is probably not only to her father as the statue that "I" despairs of patching but also to herself and her own emotional "break" approximately three years earlier. Decidedly, this poem anticipates the later "Daddy," in which the Colossus figure is expanded to include also the husband, and wherein the poet has abandoned her patching efforts. In "The Colossus," the speaker contends that

> Thirty years not I have laboured
> To dredge the silt from your throat.
> I am none the wiser.
>
> Scaling little ladders with gluepots and pails of lysol
> I crawl like an ant in mourning
> Over the weedy acres of your brow.

But in "Daddy," she announces that "I have had to kill you." Still praying for recovery in the early work, she continues in "The Colossus":

> A blue sky out of the Oresteia
> Arches above us. O father, all by yourself
> You are pithy and historical as the Roman Forum.

Identifying with Orestes in this poem, she reaches for another parallel in "Electra on Azalea Path":

> I borrow the stilts of an old tragedy.
> The truth is, one late October, at my birth-cry
> A scorpion stung its head, an ill-starred thing;

> My mother dreamed you face down in the sea.
>
> . . . . . . . . . . . . . . . . . . . . . . . . . . . . . . .
>
> O pardon the one who knocks for pardon at
> Your gate, father—your hound-bitch, daughter, friend.
> It was my love that did us both to death.[23]

And in "The Eye-Mote," she uses still another, similar classical reference to describe the conflict:

> I wear the present itch for flesh,
> Blind to what will be and what was.
> I dream that I am Oedipus.
>
> What I want back is what I was
> Before the bed, before the knife.

This Orestes-Electra-Oedipus person is surely the one who speaks so powerfully in such later poems as not only "Daddy" but also "Fever 103°," "Lady Lazarus," and "Little Fugue."

Indeed, this ominous Colossus figure is represented relatively early in Sylvia Plath's work. Her award-winning short story, "Sunday at the Mintons'," published in 1952 at the end of her sophomore year in college, concerns the relationship of Elizabeth Minton with her brother Henry, "a colossus astride the roaring sea." The maiden Elizabeth has returned to her family home by the ocean to care for her older brother in his retirement. She has, apparently, always been dominated and bullied by him; orderly, demanding, and overbearing, Henry scorns Elizabeth's active imagination and her tendency to daydream. Now that she and Henry are together again, Elizabeth instinctively reverts to her childhood role: "a little girl, obedient and yielding."[24] Yet she finds growing within her a new attitude of defiance. In the story's denouement, Elizabeth imagines that as she and Henry take their prescribed walk near the sea following Sunday's dinner, Henry is drowned. One thing that is particularly interesting here is the cause of Henry's demise; he is doing a favor for Elizabeth—retrieving a pin she has dropped—when the sea overcomes him. Elizabeth's response to this cataclysmic event is also significant; she watches for a time in wonder, almost in delight, before she steps to join Henry in the stormy waves. Her ambivalence is complete;

she is at once defiant and yielding. Elizabeth, the little girl figure, may bring death to the colossus, but she must ultimately also join him in death.

An additional contributor to these conflicts so clearly expressed in Plath's early work is the mother. This is of especial interest because Plath mentions her mother very little in her late poetry. The principal maternal figure in *Ariel* is the poet herself, and mother-child relationships are treated there in a loving, poignant way quite different from the modes of expression in *Colossus*.

In a number of the poems that make up "Poem for a Birthday," the mother's relation to the speaker, as the speaker comprehends and shapes it, appears generally distant and unconcerned. The poem "Maenad" seems central in defining these individuals and their relationship, for the speaker does assume the character of a maenadic woman, frenzied and raging, throughout the seven-poem sequence. And the cause of the speaker's present condition is assigned, in "Maenad," largely to maternal disregard:

> The mother of mouths didn't love me.
> The old man shrank to a doll.
> O I am too big to go backward:
> . . . . . . . . . . . . . . . . . . . . . . . .
> Mother, keep out of my barnyard,
> I am becoming another.[25]

In a different tone, the poem "The Disquieting Muses" deals also, and in detail, with mother. The speaker addresses her imaginary poem-mother directly in a series of stanzas each designed to explore a particular aspect of the daughter's childhood recollections. Generally, the poet expresses here the familiar you-don't-understand-me theme of nearly every child to a parent, of nearly every daughter to a mother. But one suspects that for this speaker (as for many others), the strength of the conviction is not diminished by its lack of uniqueness. And we see operating here as well the poet's modification of circumstances to communicate emotional truth. Plath's real mother's comments about the poem underscore the point. While remarking on Sylvia's "tendency to fuse characters and manipulate events to achieve her own artistic ends," Aurelia Plath calls attention to several biographical and factual inaccuracies in "The Disquieting Muses." In Aurelia's view, these inaccuracies, these " 'violation[s] of actual circumstances' " (as she quotes Richard

Wilbur), result from Sylvia's tendency to "achieve release when troubled by writing things out, thereby dissipating her frustration":[26]

> Mother, mother, what illbred aunt
> Or what disfigured and unsightly
> Cousin did you so unwisely keep
> Unasked to my christening, that she
> Sent these ladies in her stead
> With heads like darning-eggs to nod
> And nod and nod at foot and head
> And at the left side of my crib?
>
> Day now, night now, at head, side, feet,
> They stand their vigil in gowns of stone,
> Faces blank as the day I was born,
> Their shadows long in the setting sun
> That never brightens or goes down.
> And this is the kingdom you bore me to,
> Mother, mother. But no frown of mine
> Will betray the company I keep.

Further, of course, in the poems "The Colossus," "Electra on Azalea Path," and "The Eye-Mote," the daughter-father relationship is invoked together with the daughter-mother relationship as a source of conflict. Orestes, with whom the poet identifies, murdered his mother with the assistance of Electra, his sister; Oedipus' incestuous love for his mother occasioned her death.

Thus, these poems present not only an early statement of the poet's ambivalent sexual attitudes, they foreshadow the later poems in other ways as well. As Charles Newman observes, "clearly the loss of the father, the ambiguous hand of the mother will remain her central preoccupations."[27] "The Eye-Mote," especially, should be read partly as a metaphor for Plath's peculiar, surreal vision, which operates only erratically in the early poems but persistently in the late ones:

> Blameless as daylight I stood looking
> At a field of horses, necks bent, manes blown

> Tails streaming against the green
> Backdrop of sycamores.
> . . . . . . . . . . . . . . . . . . . . . . . . . . . . . . . .
> When the splinter flew in and stuck in my eye,
> Needling it dark. Then I was seeing
> A melding of shapes in a hot rain:
> Horses warped on the altering green,
>
> Outlandish as double-humped camels or unicorns,
> Grazing at the margins of a bad monochrome,
> Beasts of oasis, a better time.
> Abrading my lid, the small grain burns:
> Red cinder around which I myself
> Horses, planets and spires revolve.

The horses of this poem strongly suggest the horse Ariel galloping toward the still point, toward "What I want," toward death.

The source of the conflicts expressed in these poems is mainly sexual, and the manifestations of this dilemma are far-reaching. The poems' speakers long to be a "strumpet," a "foul slut": "Until every man, / Red, pale or dark, / Veers to her slouch" ("Strumpet Song"). She yearns for the sexual abandon offered by the fantastic snakecharmer who "Pipes water green until green waters waver / With reedy lengths and necks and undulatings" ("Snakecharmer"). Yet her "present itch for flesh" ("The Eye-Mote") conflicts with the "Spinster" in her:

> And round her house she set
> Such a barricade of barb and check
> Against mutinous weather
> As no mere insurgent man could hope to break
> With curse, fist, threat,
> Or love, either.

Even the tone of this poem is uncertain, thereby illustrating the conflict between strumpet and spinster shown so clearly among the other poems and in *The Bell Jar.*

## Integration

There seems to exist a positive correlation between the poet's increasingly honest confrontation with these problems and a growing power and efficiency in her poetry; extraneous props like a cuckoo clock, a staircase, or frivolous gothicism in nature give way to mythic reference, and strumpets, stones, snakes, and spinsters are as symbolic and internal as they are real. The few poems in this early group in which Plath controls together many or all of the facets of her personal dilemma instead of creating artificial divisions in it anticipate the later poetry. In "Full Fathom Five," Plath writes:

> Old man, you surface seldom.
> Then you come in with the tide's coming
>
> . . . . . . . . . . . . . . . . . . . . . . . . . . . . . . .
>
> All obscurity
> Starts with a danger:
> Your dangers are many. I
> Cannot look much but your form suffers
> Some strange injury
>
> And seems to die. . . .

This poem, and several of the others quoted above, demonstrate the structural freedom and verbal elasticity of the mature, later work. "The Stones," the last poem in the "Poem for a Birthday" sequence and in *The Colossus*, attests to Plath's achievement of that style:

> This is the city where men are mended.
> I lie on a great anvil.
>
> . . . . . . . . . . . . . . . . . . . . . . . . . . . . . . .
>
> Love is the bone and sinew of my curse.
> The vase, reconstructed, houses
> The elusive rose.
>
> Ten fingers shape a bowl for shadows.
> My mendings itch. There is nothing to do.
> I shall be as good as new.

"The Stones," then, represents both a culmination and a departure, a success afforded by the "advanced exercises" of the earlier poems. Ted Hughes also sees "The Stones" as a turning point in Plath's poetic career: "THE STONES was the last poem she wrote . . . in America. The immediate source of it was a series of poems she began as a deliberate exercise in experimental improvisation on set themes. She had never in her life improvised. The powers that compelled her to write so slowly had always been stronger than she was. But quite suddenly she found herself free to let herself drop, rather than inch over bridges of concepts." "The Stones" "is clearly enough the first eruption of the voice that produced *Ariel*."[28]

# Chapter Six

# Transitional Poetry

If "The Stones" is the "first eruption" of that final, excellent voice, however, it does not herald immediate success. There are a number of poems Plath wrote between 1959, the year before publication of *The Colossus*, and early 1962 that may be accurately termed transitional. These poems, collected in *Crossing the Water* and designated "transitional poems" on the volume's title page, belong to the three-year period that followed Plath's second visit to England. This was the time of the Hugheses' two years in London and their first year in Devon, an interval ending sometime near the breakup of their marriage and Ted's departure from home. It was not, on the whole, either a happy or a productive time for Plath. To be sure, her two children were born in these years—Frieda Rebecca in 1960, and Nicholas Farrar in 1962. But it was a time when Plath often felt choked by domesticity, as she said, and when she suffered continuing poor health.

The poems that we may call transitional generally reveal neither the honesty of the early poems nor the power of the late ones. To be sure, a number of poems that properly belong to Plath's late period were written also during 1960–1962; the distinction between "transitional" and "late" must be made on the basis not only of composition date but also of style and approach. Indeed, the transitional volume *Crossing the Water* is aptly named, for the poems of this period do evince, variously, a kind of stepping-stone quality, or a sense of floundering, of being neither on one shore nor the other. At the same time, they also represent an important stage in Plath's poetic development.

In the interest of accuracy, it should be noted both that the *Crossing the Water* poems were collected and published by Plath's estate eight years after her death and that, like the early volume *Colossus*, the contents of the American and British editions differ slightly. The 10 early poems not included in the American *Colossus* are printed in the American version of *Crossing the Water*. And there are six transitional poems in the English volume that do not appear in the American. These poems—"Pheasant," "An Appearance," "Event," "Apprehensions," "The Tour," and "Among the Narcissi"—are included instead in the American edition of *Winter Trees*. By their nature, however, these six poems seem to belong to Plath's transitional period, and they shall be treated here as such.

We can date the composition of these 33 transitional poems with the aid of *Crystal Gazer* and *Lyonnesse* (both published in 1971), the "Six Poems" published in *The New Yorker* in 1971, the poems that appear in the appendix to *The Art of Sylvia Plath*, and the table of contents of *The Collected Poems*. According to these sources (whose information again conflicts in a few instances), "Private Ground" and "Poem for a Birthday" were composed in 1959; "Stillborn," "On Deck," Sleep in the Mojave Desert," "Leaving Early," "Love Letter," "Magi," "Candles," "A Life," and "Two Campers in Cloud Country" were written in 1960; "Parliament Hill Fields," "Whitsun," "I Am Vertical," "Insomniac," "Wuthering Heights," "Blackberrying," "Finisterre," "The Surgeon at 2 A.M.," "Face Lift," "Heavy Women," "The Babysitters," "In Plaster," "Widow," "Mirror," "Zoo Keeper's Wife," and "Last Words" were composed in 1961; and "Among the Narcissi," "The Tour," "Pheasant," "An Appearance," and "Apprehensions" were written in 1962.

## Structural Transitions

Plath's transitional work reveals, in several ways, the poet's continuing quest to achieve her own style. For one thing, the stepping-stone quality of these transitional poems is revealed in their structure; the mutation in Plath's use of rhymes, rhythms, sounds, and stanza forms from the early to the late poems is a process instructive to follow in tracing her gradual achievement of economical expression. John Frederick Nims accurately, and closely, describes the differences in these specific components in the *Colossus* and *Ariel* poems; he observes a "less obtrusive" attention to sound effects and at the same time a stronger emphasis on "ghostly," irregular end rhymes in *Ariel*, a more obvious attention to short stanzas combined with a near abandonment of formal end-rhyme and stanza constructions, and a change from metrical experimentation in *Colossus* to an almost exclusive use of iambs in *Ariel*.[1]

We can see these changes occurring in the transitional poems. In stanza form, the early poems are far more conventionally structured than the late, and a partial survey simply of the kinds of stanza structures Plath progressively employs reveals the tendency of her poetry toward greater structural freedom and verbal elasticity. For example, in the early poems there are five villanelles and one sestina, but there are none among the transitional or late works. Further, in *The Colossus*, 12 poems are written in three-line stanzas of which six are terza rima. In *Crossing the Water*, of seven poems written in three-line stanzas, only three are terza rima. In *Ariel*, there are no terza rima constructions in the 11 poems written in three-line stanzas. Throughout her work, then, Plath seems comfortable writing in three-line stanzas; she retains this structure but moves away from her early employment of the highly schematized terza rima and villanelle toward use of a freer three-line form.

This movement toward flexibility and brevity can be dramatized also by simply cataloging different stanza lengths in Plath's early, transitional, and late work. *The Colossus* contains one poem written in two-line units with irregular end-rhyme; *Crossing the Water* has none; *Ariel* has nine. In *The Colossus* there are 11 poems in four-line stanzas, 8 poems in five-line stanzas, and 17 poems in stanzas of six or more lines; *Crossing the Water* contains no four-line and six five-line stanza poems, and 20 poems in stanzas of six or more lines; in *Ariel*, 3 of the poems are written in four-line stanzas, 15 in five-line, and only 5 in stanzas of six or more lines. After experimentation in long stanzas, then, Plath generally returns in her late work to shorter, more economical, and more flexible stanza forms.

The trend is toward a simpler, more direct, and more emphatic verse. This same trend may be observed in Plath's use of rhythms and diction. Nims observes that whereas the predominant metrical pattern of *The Colossus* is the syllabic line, the nearly exclusive pattern in *Ariel* is the iambic. The poems in *Crossing the Water* are written in the earlier mode. The diction of *Colossus*, says Nims, "is always distinguished and elegant" but is "a written language rather than a spoken one." In *Ariel*, on the other hand, we hear "a real voice in a real body in a real world."[2] Again, *Crossing the Water* belongs more to the *Colossus* than to the *Ariel* category.

This change in Plath's poems from a written to a spoken language is one observed not only by a number of critics but also by the poet herself. Douglas Cleverdon suggests that Plath's composition of the voice play *Three Women*, and her experience in broadcasting this and other poetry over the BBC from 1960 on, may well have marked the turning point between poems not meant to be read aloud and poems intended to be.[3] A. Alvarez, too, observes a difference "between finger-count" in Plath's early poems and "ear-count" in the late; "one measures the rhythm by rules," he contends, whereas "the other catches the movement by the inner disturbance it creates."[4] On this subject, we may indeed invoke the poet herself, who, in a 1962 interview and reading of her own work, claimed that designing her poems to be effective when read aloud "is something I didn't do in my earlier poems. For example, my first book, *The Colossus*, I can't read any of the poems aloud now. I didn't write them to be read aloud. . . . These ones . . . that are very recent, I've got to say them, I speak them to myself and I think that this in my own writing development is quite a new thing with me, and whatever lucidity they may have comes from the fact that I say them to myself, I say them aloud."[5]

This observation is certainly accurate. Because of their syntax, for one thing, a number of Plath's early poems yield very reluctantly to being read aloud. The Petrarchan sonnet "Mayflower" (1955) offers one example of this unwieldy syntactical aspect in the early work. In it, the occasional dropping of the definite and indefinite articles lends a jerky, abrupt quality to the line flow—not the calculated, effective abruptness of such late poems as "Lady Lazarus," but a disrupting jerkiness that requires distracting pauses in the reading:

> Throughout black winter the red haws withstood
> Assault of snow-flawed winds from the dour skies
> And, bright as blood-drops, proved no brave branch dies
> If root's firm-fixed and resolution good.[6]

Other early poems, such as "Wreath for a Bridal" (1956), offer either a similar sort of disruptive ellipsis, or unexpected syntactical inversions, so that the reader becomes at times unsure of the function of certain words: "Now speak some sacrament to parry scruple / For wedlock wrought within love's proper chapel."[7] "The Goring" (1956) offers similar difficulty: "Arena dust rusted by four bulls' blood to a dull redness, / . . . / Instinct for art began with the bull's horn lofting in the mob's / Hush a lumped man-shape."[8] This crowding of words and figures that requires such deliberate, careful reading is, of course, not in itself a flawed technique. Such a poetic style can be highly effective—as used, for example, by Dylan Thomas. But, although Plath experiments with this technique in her early work, she later discards it for a more natural, spoken cadence. By the time of the transitional poems, Plath employs a much smoother syntax.

This change in oral quality from Plath's early to her late work is observable not only in the poems' syntax but in their employment of diction and sound as well. As Nims points out, "the sound of words—

any page of Sylvia Plath shows her preoccupation with it. *The Colossus* shows a concern almost excessive, unless we see it as a preparation for *Ariel*."[9] In this aspect as in most of the others, the *Crossing the Water* poems indicate transition. A reader is almost constantly aware in the early poems of technical experimentation, especially in sound (and in related diction); there, sound effects are often effective and impressive, but often obtrusive as well:

> And he within this snakedom

> Rules the writhings which make manifest
> His snakehood and his might with plaint tunes
> From his thin pipe.

> Hard gods were there, nothing else.
> Still he thumbed out something else.
> Thumbed no stony, horny pot,
> But a certain meaning green.[10]

By the time of the late poems, this tongue-twisting quality is abandoned; diction is more natural, words are more easily spoken, sound effects are more appropriate, and the line-flow is more economical. This change is already occurring in the transitional poems. There, Plath continues her experimentation with internal rhymes, and with alliteration, assonance, and consonance. But the effects throughout are less obtrusive than in the earlier poems—sometimes only slightly less so, as in the transitional "Insomniac":

> The night sky is only a sort of carbon paper,
> Blueblack, with the much-poked periods of stars
> Letting in the light, peephole after peephole—
> A bonewhite light, like death, behind all things.[11]

and more often decidedly less so, as in "Event":

> The moonlight, that chalk cliff
> In whose rift we lie

Back to back. I hear an owl cry
From its cold indigo.[12]

This transitional experimentation points toward two very different aural aspects of the late poems; Plath's increasing control over her sound effects in *Crossing the Water* allows not only the powerful subtlety of such late poems as "The Moon and the Yew Tree" or "Little Fugue" but also the effective and obvious rhymes of such poems as "Lady Lazarus" and "Daddy."

## Cut-Paper People

In all aspects of form, then, the transitional poems reveal the changes from the early to the late ones. At the same time, many seem peculiarly lifeless. Indeed, what is significant about them is their very quality of literariness and of falseness to real experience. Though it is true that the early poems seem often artificially contrived, they nonetheless manage to evince sometimes a kind of raw force. It is not the disciplined, controlled power of the late poems, in which, to quote Richard Wilbur's comment on poetry in general, "the strength of the genie comes of his being confined in a bottle."[13] But a real voice does break through in such early poems as "The Stones," "Full Fathom Five," "The Eye-Mote," and "Two Views of a Cadaver Room." We hear this real voice seldom in *Crossing the Water*.

The title poem of this transitional collection seems to express the nature of the whole group. It begins:

Black lake, black boat, two black, cut-paper people.
Where do the black trees go that drink here?
Their shadows must cover Canada.

Like the figures described in this scene, "Crossing the Water" seems colorless, two-dimensional, cut-from-paper. Clearly, Plath's ability, new-found in her composition of "The Stones," to "let herself drop, rather than inch over bridges of concepts," has not yet emerged as a consistent impulse. About the *Colossus* poems one might say that the forced, stylized quality results from the poet's vigorous experimentation with the materials of her craft. In the transitional poems, however, the lack of spontaneity appears to result rather from a certain self-consciousness on the poet's part.

Helen Vendler makes a similar observation. "The withdrawal of affect," she writes, "annihilates not only nature but people." She uses the examples of "Two Campers in Cloud Country" and "Whitsun" to show that people are no more than "stick-figures," and she comments further that "Face-Lift" reveals a "falseness to the wellsprings of life from which metaphors are drawn." The main problem with the poems in this volume, says Vendler, is that "an undeniable intellect allegorizes the issues before they are allowed expression."[14]

Two manifestations of this self-conscious intellectualizing in *Crossing the Water* are the poetry's surprisingly undramatic quality and the comparatively large number of landscape poems. In both the earlier and the later poetry, the speaker assumes an identifiable voice, an individual identity, so that the poems themselves present a clear dramatic situation. In *The Colossus*, for example, we hear the voice of a woman agonizingly confronting the sirens' temptation, or the voice of a daughter trying to come to terms with a very specific father relationship, or the voice of a proliferating mushroom family, or the voice of a spinster shakily committed to self-denial. Even in the landscape poems, such as "Hardcastle Crags" or "Point Shirley," the speaker is given a special identity and is surrounded by a particular, believable landscape for a specific and evident reason.

In *Ariel*, the same dramatic concreteness prevails. Here, there are virtually no landscape poems in the earlier sense of an identifiable natural setting for the speaker's activities. For by this time, external settings have become internalized, so that they serve only as functions of the speaker's unique vision. (For example, moonlight in "The Moon and the Yew Tree" becomes "the light of the mind," and golden apples and leaves and flowers in "Letter in November" are "the mouths of Thermopylae.") And throughout the volume, the identifiable speaker acts and talks in a clear dramatic context—a Jew victimized by a Nazi, for example, or a mother poignantly warning her child of his probable fate, or an onion-chopping housewife cutting her thumb.

But in *Crossing the Water*, we find very little dramatic concreteness and hear mainly an amorphous voice, as evinced, for example, in the first stanza of "Magi":

> The abstracts hover like dull angels:
> Nothing so vulgar as a nose or eye
> Bossing the ethereal blanks of their face-ovals.

Here as elsewhere in the volume, the poet seems sharply conscious of herself so that her poems' characters and situations remain more or less abstract.

Further, there are among these transitional works more landscape poems than appear proportionately in the work of the other periods. In them, the speaker is "I," and "I" is occasionally accompanied by "you." Generally one has the impression that "I" and "you" and the surrounding landscape exist to express an idea the poet has—an idea that, struggling for expression, renders the specifics of the poem subordinate and lifeless. In "Wuthering Heights," for instance, both speaker and landscape display a substanceless quality:

> The horizons ring me like faggots,
> Tilted and disparate, and always unstable.
> Touched by a match, they might warm me,
> And their fine lines singe
> The air to orange
> Before the distances they pin evaporate,
> Weighting the pale sky with a solider colour.
> But they only dissolve and dissolve
> Like a series of promises, as I step forward.

In "Two Campers in Cloud Country," in which the idea is the person's desire for self-effacement in an indifferent landscape, effacement occurs even before identity can be established:

> Well, one wearies of the Public Gardens: one wants a vacation
> Where trees and clouds and animals pay no notice;
> . . . . . . . . . . . . . . . . . . . . . . . . . . . . . . . . . . . .
> The Pilgrims and Indians might never have happened.
> Planets pulse in the lake like bright amoebas;
> The pines blot our voices up in their lightest sighs.

Similarly, characters fail to become real beings in a number of the other poems of *Crossing the Water*. "A Life," for example, seems to have both speaker and listener—someone is giving various orders to someone else—but we remain unsure of who they are or what they are doing or why they are doing it:

> Touch it: it won't shrink like an eyeball,
> This egg-shaped bailiwick, clear as a tear.
> . . . . . . . . . . . . . . . . . . . . . . . . . . . . . .
> Flick the glass with your fingernail:
> It will ping like a Chinese chime in the slightest air stir
> Though nobody in there looks up or bothers to answer.

An interesting companion to these observations is the fact that these transitional poems are quite humorless. We cannot be certain whether this characteristic is a cause or an effect of overintellectualization and lack of spontaneity; it is observable, however, that with a very few exceptions, these poems lack the wit, the drollery, and even the bitter, mocking humor of both the early and the late work. To be sure, there is a witty line or two, for example in "Leaving Early": "Lady, your room is lousy with flowers." And we can hear the humorous satire of the early poem "A Winter's Tale" in the transitional "On Deck":

> The untidy lady revivalist
> For whom the good Lord provides (He gave
> Her a pocketbook, a pearl hatpin
> And seven winter coats last August)
> Prays under her breath that she may save
> The art students in West Berlin.

or the mocking tones of early and late poems in "The Tour":

> O maiden aunt, you have come to call.
> Do step into the hall!
> . . . . . . . . . . .
> And *this*
> Is where I kept the furnace,
> . . . . . . . . . . . . . . . . . . .
> It simply exploded one night,
> It went up in smoke.
> And that's why I have no hair, auntie, that's why I choke.[15]

As a group, however, the transitional poems are quite sober.

Another poem in *Crossing the Water* that seems expressive of the whole group of transitional poems is "Stillborn," in which the poet herself announces her dissatisfaction with her work:

> These poems do not live: it's a sad diagnosis.
> They grew their toes and fingers well enough,
> Their little foreheads bulged with concentration.
> If they missed out on walking about like people
> It wasn't for any lack of mother-love.
>
> O I cannot understand what happened to them!
> They are proper in shape and number and every part.
> They sit so nicely in the pickling fluid!
> They smile and smile and smile and smile at me.
> And still the lungs won't fill and the heart won't start.

## Refinement of Imagery

But even though the poems of this volume may show less life and humor than the early or late poems, they are valuable not only as formal transitions but as transitions in their use of imagery as well. In this group of poems, Plath seems to have culled from the early work the relatively small group of images she will use later, and here she uses them over and over again in various combinations. One might speculate that without this time to become totally familiar with her system of imagery, she might not have succeeded in using it as brilliantly as she does in the poems that follow.

In the poem "Private Ground," for example, we find an explanation, clearer probably than any in *Ariel*, of the meaning of the familiar death images of frost, glitter, and reflection:

> All morning, with smoking breath, the handyman
> Has been draining the goldfish ponds.
> They collapse like lungs,
> . . . . . . . . . . . . . . . . . . . . . . . . . . . . . . . . . . . .
> I bend over this drained basin where the small fish
> Flex as the mud freezes.

They glitter like eyes, and I collect them all.
Morgue of old logs and old images, the lake
Opens and shuts, accepting them among its reflections.

The mirror, too, is an image that belongs to this particular group of death figures. Plath uses it in conjunction with the color white (another, related figure for death's blankness) in "Last Words": "My mirror is clouding over— / A few more breaths, and it will reflect nothing at all. / The flowers and faces whiten to a sheet." And in the poem "Mirror," Plath offers a detailed exploration of the special connotations this image has for her. We can recognize here the particular relation with death (and drowning) of such figures and allusions as candlelight and moonlight, silver, water, and narcissi:

> I am silver and exact. I have no preconceptions.
> . . . . . . . . . . . . . . . . . . . . . . . . . . . . . . . . .
> Now I am a lake. A woman bends over me,
> Searching my reaches for what she really is.
> Then she turns to those liars, the candles or the moon.
> I see her back, and reflect it faithfully.
> . . . . . . . . . . . . . . . . . . . . . . . . . . . . . . . . . . .
> Each morning it is her face that replaces the darkness.
> In me she has drowned a young girl, and in me an old woman
> Rises toward her day after day, like a terrible fish.

Related to the effacement imagery of water, and of whiteness and blankness, is the mythological allusion to Lethe, used so effectively in the late poems "Amnesiac" and "Getting There":

> Planets pulse in the lake like bright amoebas;
> The pines blot our voices up in their lightest sighs.
>
> Around our tent the old simplicities sough
> Sleepily as Lethe, trying to get in.
> We'll wake blank-brained as water in the dawn.
>                         ("Two Campers in Cloud Country")

Further, "Face-Lift," a poem where the woman's face-lift operation sounds very much like suicide, shows clearly, and for the first time, the reincarnation image so common in *Ariel*: "Mother to myself, I wake swaddled in gauze, / Pink and smooth as a baby."

And the saint-sinner conflict, so thematically central to the early poetry, is evident in this transitional work as well but with a significant difference. Whereas in the *Colossus* poems Plath chose to express this split in separate, opposing poems ("Spinster" versus "Strumpet Song," for instance), here she expresses it within a single poem, "In Plaster":

> I shall never get out of this! There are two of me now:
> This new absolutely white person and the old yellow one,
> And the white person is certainly the superior one.
> She doesn't need food, she is one of the real saints.
>
> . . . . . . . . . . . . . . . . . . . . . . . . . . . . . . . . . . . . . . . . . . . .
>
> I used to think we might make a go of it together—
> After all, it was a kind of marriage, being so close.
> Now I see it must be one or the other of us.
> She may be a saint, and I may be ugly and hairy,
> But she'll soon find out that that doesn't matter a bit.
> I'm collecting my strength; one day I shall manage without her,
> And she'll perish with emptiness then, and begin to miss me.

This technique of manifesting conflicting aspects of the self within a single speaker emphasizes the desperate, intense aspect of the split. And after experimenting with this technique in "In Plaster," Plath skillfully reemploys it in such late poems as "Lesbos" and "Fever 103°."

## Toward *Ariel*

Plath's transitional poems, then, are developmentally significant in several ways. And in this light, even their failures are important, for they reveal the poet's continuing efforts to shape the materials of her craft to her special use, to find her own voice. Furthermore, it would be inaccurate to imply that there are not some very fine poems among them. In a few instances, Plath seems not to have been able to maintain the intellectual defenses that denied life and power to so many of these transitional poems, and she created instead the direct, affecting kind of poem that was to become the predominant mode of the final work.

One of these poems is "Private Ground." Outstanding for its skillful use of sound and rhythm, this poem reflects the change in oral quality from Plath's early to her late work; it catches the reader's attention in the cadences of the very first line: "First frost, and I walk among the rosefruit," and continues throughout to evince a very readable and spoken texture.

Another fine poem in *Crossing the Water* is "Blackberrying." Belonging to the landscape tradition of such earlier poems as "Point Shirley" and "Watercolor of Grantchester Meadows" and of so many transitional poems, this work shows one direction Plath's verse was going:

> Nobody in the lane, and nothing, nothing but blackberries,
> Blackberries on either side, though on the right mainly,
> A blackberry alley, going down in hooks, and a sea
> Somewhere at the end of it, heaving.

The plain description of the external landscape in this poem is powerful and lively. But beyond that, rhythms and word sounds afford to the experience a distorted quality suggesting that this landscape is internal as well:

> Blackberries
> Big as the ball of my thumb, and dumb as eyes
> Ebon in the hedges, fat
> With blue-red juices. These they squander on my fingers.
> I had not asked for such a blood sisterhood; they must love me.
> They accommodate themselves to my milkbottle,
> flattening their sides.

"The Surgeon at 2 A.M." shows a similar and more pronounced external-internal distortion. Performing his operation in a white, sterile environment, the surgeon describes a procedure belonging more to the nightmare (appropriately, the time is 2:00 A.M.) than to the operating room:

> The white light is artificial, and hygienic as heaven.
> The microbes cannot survive it.

They are departing in their transparent garments, turned aside
From the scalpels and the rubber hands.
The scalded sheet is now a snowfield, frozen and peaceful.
The body under it is in my hands.
As usual there is no face. A lump of Chinese white
With seven holes thumbed in.

Notice, too, the imagery of white, cold, and freezing, of flowers, color, and blooming, of hooks (specifically used in "Blackberrying" as well), and of perfection, so familiar in the later poems:

It is a garden I have to do with—tubers and fruits
Oozing their jammy substances,
A mat of roots. My assistants hook them back.
Stenches and colours assail me.
This is the lung-tree.
These orchids are splendid. They spot and coil like snakes.
The heart is a red-bell-bloom, in distress.
. . . . . . . . . . . . . . . . . . . . . . . . . . . . .
The blood is a sunset. I admire it.
I am up to my elbows in it, red and squeaking,
Still it seeps up, it is not exhausted.
So magical! A hot spring
I must seal off and let fill
The intricate, blue piping under this pale marble.
. . . . . . . . . . . . . . . . . . . . . . . . . . . . . . . . .
It is a statue the orderlies are wheeling off.
I have perfected it.

In the speaker's cool fascination with fantastic, horrible events, this poem is as excellent as any in the *Ariel* collection.

Finally, in "Widow" (1961) a number of major motifs from the early poems are drawn together and treated with brutal honesty; problems with father, sex, love, despair, and frustration meld with the poet's intense energy and skill to produce, truly, "the first eruption of the voice that produced *Ariel*." The poem poignantly records the sensations of rejection, loneliness, and loss that may have reflected Plath's own feelings at the time about her failing marriage. And it also succeeds in presenting the drained voice and the bare confrontation with the void that are such compelling qualities in the late poetry. The poem's first two stanzas, in a calm, almost exhausted mood, begin with these lines: "Widow. The word consumes itself— / . . . / Widow. The dead syllable, with its shadow / Of an echo. . . ." Intensity builds in stanzas three and four as the mood shifts gradually from numbness to animosity and the poet confuses husband with father:

> Widow. The bitter spider sits
> And sits in the center of her loveless spokes.
> Death is the dress she wears, her hat and collar.
> The moth-face of her husband, moonwhite and ill,
> Circles her like a prey she'd love to kill
>
> A second time, to have him near again—

And the intensity reaches its climax in stanza five:

> Widow: that great, vacant estate!
> The voice of God is full of draughtiness,
> Promising simply the hard stars, the space
> Of immortal blankness between stars.

The intensity begins to subside as animosity recedes: "Widow, the compassionate trees bend in, / The trees of loneliness, the trees of mourning." The poem closes in relative calm as the poet expresses her sense of helpless isolation:

> A bodiless soul could pass another soul
> In this clear air and never notice it—
> One soul pass through the other, frail as smoke
> And utterly ignorant of the way it took.
>
> This is the fear she has—the fear
> His soul may beat and be beating at her dull sense

Like blue Mary's angel, dovelike against a pane
Blinded to all but the grey, spiritless room
It looks in on, and must go on looking in on.

The special combination of desperation and restraint, of power and control so striking in the final poems is evident here. Still, the poems of this transitional period are relatively subdued compared with those in *Ariel* and *Winter Trees,* subdued indeed because of their special, and necessary, transitional aspect. In the poetry of *Crossing the Water*, Plath's technique is in the process of becoming, of developing from an experimental to a finely honed and natural mode. It is in the transitional work that the change in oral quality occurs, so that we see, in the individual poems of this period, the shift in her verse from a written to a spoken language. Moreover, the poet's self-consciousness, responsible for the mediocrity of so many of these transitional poems, is perhaps a necessary qualification for the precision of the late work; here, the poet comes to know herself so that her attitudes can be expressed rather than explained in her final poetry.

For there, in the poems of *Winter Trees* and *Ariel*, there is little search for new meaning and no self-pity whatever. The writing in the late poems exudes a sense of feverish necessity whose motivation is, as Stephen Spender observes, "pure need of expression."[16] Indeed, Plath herself announces there that "The blood jet is poetry, / There is no stopping it."[17]

# Chapter Seven

# Late Poetry

Collected in the posthumous volumes *Ariel* and *Winter Trees*, most of these poems belong to the last year of the poet's life, a period bounded by the birth of her son, Nicholas, in January 1962, and her suicide in February 1963. That year was a time of both great personal upheaval and great creative productivity for Plath. After her husband left her in the summer of 1962, she lived for a time alone with her two children in their Devon home before moving in December to London to seek a new life. Her health was poor; both in Devon and in London, she fought the combined hardships of flu, high fever, and cold weather. Yet she wrote more urgently than ever before; she daily set aside the early morning hours for her poetry, composing, as she said, "a poem a day before breakfast."

The principal characteristic of Plath's last poems, and what distinguishes them from the poems of her transitional period, is their innate intensity combined with their ease of composition. In this late work, composed so rapidly, Plath had indeed found her own voice, or as Ted Hughes observes in "The Chronological Order of Sylvia Plath's Poems," "She had arrived . . . at her own centre of gravity." Abandoning her customary method of working slowly and laboriously, with a thesaurus close at hand, to compose her poems, Plath now wrote "at top speed, as one might write an urgent letter."[1] All of the poems Plath wrote in the last year of her life were composed in this way. A few, written a bit earlier but in similar fashion, are also appropriately included in this late group.

With the help of Hughes's notes and the poems' arrangement in *The Collected Poems*, we may date the composition of most of the *Ariel* poems. As with previous volumes, however, the information in one source occasionally conflicts with the other's. Two poems were composed in 1960, "The Hanging Man" and "You're," written in early 1960 after the Hugheses' return to England but before the birth of their daughter, Frieda, in April. "You're," according to Hughes, followed shortly after the *Colossus* poem "The Stones" and belongs to "the first eruption of the voice that produced *Ariel*." That voice is heard also in three other *Ariel* poems written within the transitional year of 1961; these are "Tulips," "Morning Song," and "The Rival." Plath wrote "Little Fugue" in early 1962.

What Hughes calls "the final phase" began in April 1962 with the composition of "Elm" and "The Moon and the Yew Tree," both of which were inspired by the immediate surroundings of the Hugheses' Devon home. Written in July 1962, "Berck-Plage" recalls the Hugheses' visit in the summer of 1961 to the French seaside resort by that name. Another group belongs to October and November of 1962. The bee poems were written first; these are "The Bee Meeting," "The Arrival of the Bee Box," "Stings," "Wintering," and "The Swarm" (a poem included in the British edition of *Winter Trees* and the American *Ariel*). Next followed 17 poems: "The Couriers," "Sheep in Fog," "The Applicant," "Lady Lazarus," "Cut," "The Night Dances," "Poppies in October," "Ariel" (the name of the horse Plath rode in Devon), "Death & Co.," "Nick and the Candlestick" (after Nicholas, Plath's son), "Gulliver," "Getting There," "Medusa," "A Birthday Present," "Letter in November," "Daddy," and "Fever 103°." "Poppies in July" and "Years" also belong to 1962. A final group of poems was written in January 1963, Plath's last month; first came "The Munich Mannequins," "Totem," and "Paralytic." Plath wrote five others—"Balloons," "Contusion," "Kindness," "Edge," and "Words"—in February just before she died.

Once again, in the manner of Plath's early and transitional volumes, the British and American versions of *Ariel* differ slightly. The American edition (1966) contains all 40 of the poems that first appeared in the British edition, plus three additional ones: "Mary's Song," "Lesbos," and "The Swarm." "The Swarm," as we have seen, belongs with the bee poems of October 1962; "Mary's Song" and "Lesbos" were written in the same year. All three of these works, which are included only in the American *Ariel*, appear in the British *Winter Trees*.

*Winter Trees*, the fourth published volume of Plath's poetry, appeared posthumously; the British edition was published in 1971 and an American edition followed the next year. With *Ariel*, *Winter Trees* represents the work of Plath's late period; indeed, as Ted Hughes has written in a prefatory note to *Winter Trees*, these poems "are all out of the batch from which the *Ariel* poems were more or less arbitrarily chosen and they were all composed in the last year of Sylvia Plath's life."[2] This is a relatively slim volume; the British edition contains 19 poems and the American, 25. To be accurate, Plath may have written at least one of the *Winter Trees* poems before her last year; the composition of "The Rabbit

Catcher" is dated in *The Collected Poems* as 1962 but in *Lyonnesse* as 1961. And as Hughes observes in his prefatory note, "Three Women: A Poem for Three Voices" (dated 1962 in *The Collected Poems*) "can be seen as a bridge between *The Colossus* and *Ariel*, both in the change of style . . . and in that it was written to be read aloud."[3]

We know that Plath wrote three of the *Winter Trees* poems in the last month of her life; *The Collected Poems* designates the year 1963 for the composition of "Child," "Gigolo," and "Mystic." *Lyonnesse* and *Crystal Gazer* also place "Lyonnesse" in 1963, although *The Collected Poems* includes it in the 1962 group. These four poems, together with "The Rabbit Catcher" and "Three Women," appear in both editions of *Winter Trees*, as does the title poem, along with "Brasilia," "Childless Woman," "Purdah," "The Courage of Shutting-Up," "The Other," "Stopped Dead," "By Candlelight," "Thalidomide," and "For a Fatherless Son." The three poems that complete the contents for the Faber *Winter Trees* are those ("Lesbos," "The Swarm," and "Mary's Song") that appear in the American *Ariel*. And the nine poems that complete the American *Winter Trees* are the six transitional poems that appeared in the British but not the American *Crossing the Water* ("Apprehensions," "An Appearance," "Among the Narcissi," "Event," "Pheasant," and "The Tour"), plus three poems that appear in no other commercial volume: "Eavesdropper," "The Detective," and "Amnesiac."

## Two *Ariels*

Let us return for a moment to Ted Hughes's remark quoted previously that the *Winter Trees* poems, "composed in the last year of Sylvia Plath's life," "are all out of a batch from which the *Ariel* poems were more or less arbitrarily chosen." Then let us turn to page 295 of *The Collected Poems* where Hughes lists the order of what he calls "Sylvia Plath's own prepared collection of poems, titled *Ariel*." At her death, Plath left her volume *Ariel* ready for publication. The contents of the volume called *Ariel* that was published two years later had undergone some change, maybe "more or less arbitrarily" and maybe not, and the poems "were . . . chosen" therefore by someone else (note the passive voice).

There are 43 poems in Harper and Row's *Ariel*, 40 in Faber's (contents identical to Harper's except for the deletion of "Lesbos," "Mary's Song," and "The Swarm"), and 41 in the *Ariel* Plath left for publication when she died. The contents of Plath's unpublished volume differ substantially from the published one: 12 of her 41 poems did not find their way into either of the 1965 *Ariel*s. These are "The Rabbit Catcher," "Thalidomide," "Barren Woman," "A Secret," "The Jailer," "The Detective," "Magi," "The Other," "Stopped Dead," "The Courage of Shutting-Up," "Purdah," and "Amnesiac." Most appeared later in *Winter Trees* or *Crossing the Water*; three ("Barren Woman, "A Secret," "The Jailer") appeared for the first time in *The Collected Poems*. And those 12 poems deleted from Plath's *Ariel* were replaced by 15 other mostly late poems: "Sheep in Fog," "Tulips," "Mary's Song," "The Hanging Man," "Little Fugue," "Years," "The Munich Mannequins," "Totem," "Paralytic," "Balloons," "Poppies in July," "Kindness," "Contusion," "Edge," "Words." Of those 15, the last 12 (beginning with "The Hanging Man") appear in the order listed as the final 12 poems of the published volume.

Plath's *Ariel* would have opened with "Morning Song" and closed with "Wintering." (In both her volume and the published one, "Ariel" appeared near the middle: 15th in Plath's *Ariel* and 12th in the published one.) Both volumes, then, begin with "Morning Song," which celebrates new life: "Love set you going like a fat gold watch." The published *Ariel* ends with "Words," written on February 1, 1963, 10 days before Plath's death, a poem of death imagery (mirror, echo, skull) and finality ("From the bottom of the pool, fixed stars / Govern a life"). Plath's intended volume, on the other hand, concludes with "Wintering," also a poem of familiar death images (white, glitter, dark enclosure) but one where the surviving bees "are all women" who "have got rid of the men" and who "will . . . survive . . . / To enter another year," for "The bees are flying. They taste the spring." Between "Love" and "spring," between themes of motherhood, betrayal, and female survival, the poems of Plath's *Ariel* tell the story of her final years, her failed marriage, her fury, her despair. But her volume moves though anger and bitterness to end with the imagery of rebirth so typical of her work. As Ted Hughes notes in his introduction to *The Collected Poems*, Plath's own "careful sequence . . . began with the word 'Love' and ended with the word 'Spring' " (*CP*, 14–15). Here is the way Hughes explains (in passive or nonattributive structure) his changes to that "careful sequence":

> The *Ariel* eventually published in 1965 was a somewhat different volume from the one she had planned. . . . It omitted some of the more personally aggressive poems from 1962, and might have omitted one or two more if she had not already published them herself in magazines. . . . The collection that appeared was my eventual compromise between publish-

ing a large bulk of her work . . . and introducing her late work more cautiously. . . . (Several advisers had felt that the violent contradictory feelings expressed in those pieces might prove hard for the reading public to take.) (*CP,* 15)

For 16 years (1965 to 1981), then, readers and scholars studied not Plath's own *Ariel* but Hughes's version of it. Learning of this deception is akin to discovering that a sonata we thought was genuine was finished by the composer's husband, who retained the composer's original notation but rearranged the ending. Although this discovery does not substantially change our evaluation of Plath's oeuvre, we nonetheless feel tricked, kept from knowing the poet's intent for 16 important years.

## Fusions

By any arrangement, however, the world of these late poems is the world of a nightmare, though there are constant objects and places in it that define its boundaries, allowing the visitor to recognize its outlines and affording the poetry much of its control. This world is made up mostly of aspects of the several worlds of the early poetry, now assimilated and working together. There are, as Stephen Spender notes, "the dark outlines of a mythology of people and places which provide the structure of the control, the landmarks among which the poetry is moving" (Spender, 23). Not only do Orestes, Oedipus, and Lethe appear in this dark mythology; others such as Cerberus, Ariel, Medusa, and various biblical characters play their part. The poet's German father figures darkly and often in reference to persons and to concentration camps. A necessary gothic moon provides the light, and the yew tree stands blackly by. Permeating these dark landmarks is the wild seascape of the poet's childhood, its recollected feel and smell as well as the emotions associated with it. All these provide at once the reserve from which the poet draws her imagery and symbolism and the referents in which meaning resides.

Indeed, Plath herself offers valuable commentary concerning the means by which private experience and sensibility are made accessible and public in these late poems. As the poet commented in an interview conducted a year before her death:

I think my poems immediately come out of the sensuous and emotional experiences I have, but I must say I cannot sympathize with these cries

from the heart that are informed by nothing except a needle or a knife.
. . . I believe that one should be able to control and manipulate experiences, even the most terrifying, like madness, being tortured, . . . with an informed and intelligent mind. I think that personal experience is very important, but certainly it shouldn't be a . . . narcissistic experience. I believe it should be *relevant,* and relevant to the larger things, the bigger things such as Hiroshima and Dachau and so on. (*TPS,* 169–70)

Thus, to adopt Plath's chosen example, a "relevant" issue like Dachau becomes in her poems an analogue for the private experience she presents. For one thing, Dachau is not merely an external, distant, politically interesting place for Plath; she admits that, because of her own paternal German and maternal Austrian origin, her "concern with concentration camps and so on is uniquely intense" (*TPS,* 169). Already, then, external-internal perimeters are being shifted; the poet's interest in Dachau is simultaneously personal and objective. And once this link between the inner and outer world is established, analogy can become metaphor. Father can become Nazi, with all of the rigidity and suppression and atrocity suggested thereby; daughter, becoming a Jewish victim, has found the natural vehicle to express her feelings of helplessness, rage, bitterness, and so forth.

In Plath's late poems, the ultimate result of this linking of the inner with the outer world is that distinctions between external and internal reality are virtually removed. Landscape exists only as the poet perceives it. In Spender's words, "The landscape is an entirely interior, mental one in which external objects have become converted into symbols of hysterical vision." Nature is as much inside the poet as it is outside of her, or "if there are some externals in these poems . . . they exist in an atmosphere where the external is in immediate process of becoming the internal, opposites identical with one another" (Spender, 25). "Getting There" serves as a good example of such internal-external fusion:

> The gigantic gorilla interior
> Of the wheels move, they appal me—
> The terrible brains
> Of Krupp, black muzzles
> Revolving, the sound

Punching out Absence! Like cannon.
. . . . . . . . . . . ... . . . . . . . . . . . . . .
There is mud on my feet,
Thick, red and slipping, It is Adam's side,
This earth I rise from, and I in agony.
I cannot undo myself, and the train is steaming.
Steaming and breathing, its teeth
Ready to roll, like a devil's.
. . . . . . . . . . . ... . . . . . . . . . . . . . . . . . . . . . . . . . . .
It is so small
The place I am getting to, why are there these obstacles—
. . . . . . . . . . . . . . . . . . . . . . . . . . . . . . . . . . . . . . .
The fire's between us.
Is there no still place
Turning and turning in the middle air,
Untouched and untouchable.
The train is dragging itself, it is screaming—
An animal
Insane for the destination,
The bloodspot,
The face at the end of the flare.[4]

The common ground on which external and internal meet and merge in
this poem is the notion of rushing—of rushing toward an established,
anticipated goal. In terms of external reality, the forward momentum
belongs to the train, carrying Nazi victims, rushing through the
countryside toward its next, or last, stop—possibly a concentration
camp. In terms of internal reality, the forward momentum belongs to a
person, one of the train's passengers and thus a victim, rushing also
toward a known terminal. The nature and quality of this journey are
defined by the surreal merging of inner and outer realities. The train's
interior and wheels are "appalling" (note the pun); the vehicle is a
gorilla, a devil with fangs, a screaming animal insane for the destination.
In this nightmare world, the victim slides and slips in thick red mud,
driven in forward motion, helpless to disembark.

Death is "the place" this passenger is "getting to," the "still place" in
most of these poems. It is part of Plath's special landscape and is

omnipresent in her set of particularized images, in which internal and external realities blend so completely that one becomes indistinguishable from the other. As A. R. Jones aptly observes, "The relationship between the inner and outer worlds is fractured, the outer world holding up a mirror in which the inner world can see its distorted self."[5] We see an interesting correlate to this process, especially in light of "Getting There," in *The Bell Jar*, when Esther Greenwood is describing a skiing experience: "I plummeted down past the zigzaggers, the students, the experts, through year after year of doubleness and smiles and compromise, into my own past. People and trees receded on either hand like the dark sides of a tunnel as I hurtled on to the still, bright point at the end of it, the pebble at the bottom of the well, the white sweet baby cradled in its mother's belly" (*B*, 108). Whether the destination is expressed in terms of still points, of dewdrops, of blood spots, of new babies, or of submerged rocks, in nearly all of the late poems the poet is indeed "getting there."

Much of this death imagery seems to grow from Plath's recollections of her sea childhood. In "Ocean 1212-W" she recalls how she could never watch her "grandmother drop the dark green lobsters . . . into the boiling pot from which they would be, in a minute, drawn—red, dead, and edible. I felt the awful scald of the water too keenly on my skin."[6] Death is red in "Getting There," as it is in easily one half of the poems in *Ariel* and *Winter Trees*:

> I am red meat.
>
> . . . . . . . . . . .
> I do not stir.
>
> The dead bell,
> The dead bell.
>
> Somebody's done for.
> ("Death & Co.")

And often death is both red and scalding:

> And I
> Am the arrow,

The dew that flies
Suicidal, at one with the drive
Into the red

Eye, the cauldron of morning.
("Ariel")

Death is also a glitter in these poems. In "Berck-Plage" in which "An old man is vanishing," "things are glittering." In "Gigolo," the speaker "glitter[s] like Fontainebleau,"[7] and the undertaker in "Death & Co." is a "Bastard/Masturbating a glitter." Mirrors glitter too, and mirrors represent death in many of the poems; in "The Courage of Shutting-Up," for example, mirrors "can kill," and in "Contusion" "the mirrors are sheeted" after "the heart shuts." Glitter goes also with the sea in Plath's association, and sea is death as well: "Even with my eyes shut I could feel the glimmers of [the sea's] bright mirrors spider over my lids." Her childhood sea was "like a deep woman, it hid a good deal; it had many faces, many delicate, terrible veils. It spoke of miracles and distances; if it could court, it could also kill." She can remember crawling into it, fascinated, before she could walk, nearly drowning.[8] And these associations become images in the late poems, for example in "A Birthday Present":

What is this, behind this veil, is it ugly, is it beautiful?
Is it shimmering, has it breasts, has it edges?
. . . . . . . . . . . . . . . . . . . . . . . . . . . . . . . . . . . . . . .
But it shimmers, it does not stop, and I think it wants me.
. . . . . . . . . . . . . . . . . . . . . . . . . . . . . . . . . . . . . . .
Only let down the veil, the veil, the veil.
If it were death

I would admire the deep gravity of it, its timeless eyes.

The landscape is a deathly landscape, then; such things as the landmarks and objects in "Getting There" and the elements of the seascape are at once objective and subjective items and conditions. Even common household objects become internalized and strange under the distorted, surreal gaze of the poet:

Viciousness in the kitchen!
The potatoes hiss,
It is all Hollywood, windowless,
The fluorescent light wincing on and off like a terrible migraine

Coy paper strips for doors—
Stage curtains, a widow's frizz.

("Lesbos")

This fusion of external and internal landscape seems, in its particular manifestations, a kind of weird, updated metaphysical conceit. Nor is this the only kind of fusion of opposites in these late poems; the opposites of love and hate are fused as well, with death as the catalyst. Even in death there is a merging of opposites, for death is at once the act of loving, the lover, and the only possible place to find love. Clearly, Plath has achieved excellence in the late works through her controlled and organic manipulation of imagery. Indeed, in a number of the *Ariel* and *Winter Trees* poems, the progressive linking of one image to the next creates a new order of reality for the whole poem in much the same way that the creating of a single metaphor makes us see differently, or more clearly.

The form of "Little Fugue," for example, is determined by the musical structure for which the poem is named. Subject and countersubject are introduced in the first stanza:

The yew's black fingers wag;
Cold clouds go over.
So the deaf and dumb
Signal the blind, and are ignored.

The subject is repeated through the poem in three more "voices": "A yew hedge of orders"; "The yew my Christ, then"; "And you, during the Great War"; so that by the time the development is ended, the black yew stands for senseless, "deaf and dumb" tyranny and oppression in its manifestations of death, Nazi father, and Christ's executioners; and the countersubject, the white cloud, stands for the innocent "blind" victim in its manifestations of featurelessness, emptiness, and pallor.

A closer look at "Mary's Song" reveals specifically how this linking of images works. The Mary of this excellent poem is at once Christ's mother and the poet herself, and sacrifice is the concept that controls specific images:

> The Sunday lamb cracks in its fat.
> The fat
> Sacrifices its opacity. . . .
>
> A window, holy gold.
> The fire makes it precious,
> The same fire
>
> Melting the tallow heretics,
> Ousting the Jews.
> Their thick palls float
>
> Over the cicatrix of Poland, burnt-out
> Germany.
> They do not die.
>
> Grey birds obsess my heart,
> Mouth-ash, ash of eye.
> They settle. On the high
>
> Precipice
> That emptied one man into space
> The ovens glowed like heavens, incandescent.
>
> It is a heart,
> This holocaust I walk in,
> O golden child the world will kill and eat.

The "Sunday lamb" cooking for dinner is also Christ, the sacrificial Lamb. As this lamb cooks, the fat on the outside of it "sacrifices its opacity," becoming crispy and golden—thereby "precious." And the same fire that kills and cooks the lamb (or the Lamb), melts his fat, and makes him precious through sacrifice, also kills the Jews (Christ was a Jew) and melts their "tallow." So that the smoke and ashes (note the several meanings of "palls") of their sacrifice can float over Germany, the home of the victimizers, suggesting a kind of resurrection that maintains the Christ parallel. Ashes from these sacrifices, as they float, settle on Mary, the survivor, reminding her of both the crucifixion and the Nazi ovens; her world is now both ashen gray and a "holocaust." And the poem's last line points in a new direction; the world has killed the lamb, the "golden child," but the process of eating it (Him) suggests the sacrament of Communion.

Certainly, the ordering and juxtaposing of images in this poem richly creates a new kind of reality. The motif of the Jew as Nazi victim belongs to the poet's personal symbology, and we remember her constant use of this image to describe herself and her condition. Her linking of this Jewish victim with Christ and with her own baby boy in this poem, and her female connection of all three victims with a roasting lamb certainly creates for the reader a new way of seeing each and all of these elements.

## Conflicts

The strumpet-spinster conflict of the early poetry and of the transitional "In Plaster" is powerfully expressed in these late poems, usually in a kind of schizoid manner within a single poem. In "The Other," for instance, "I" and "you" are irrevocably sundered; "I," the speaker, exclaims: "Cold glass, how you insert yourself / Between myself and myself. / I scratch like a cat." And in "Lesbos," strumpet and spinster assume separate identities. The device of the double we have observed elsewhere in Plath's work, most notably in *The Bell Jar*, works here as we hear a woman talking to herself. "I," the speaker, is strumpet: "I should sit on a rock off Cornwall and comb my hair. / I should wear tiger pants, I should have an affair." Yet we hear in these Prufrock-like lines a conflict even within the strumpet's consciousness. "You," the silent member of the conversation, is spinster: "You peer from the door, / Sad hag. 'Every woman's a whore. / I can't communicate.' " The breakdown of communication is irrevocable and destructive: "I call you Orphan, orphan. You are ill. / . . . / I say I may be back. / You know what lies are for." This divided woman also has a child. And in the forecast of suffering that results by extension for her baby, we recognize also the effect of this inner conflict on the mother:

> And I, love, am a pathological liar,
> And my child—look at her, face down on the floor,
> Little unstrung puppet, kicking to disappear—
> Why she is schizophrenic,
>
> . . . . . . . . . . . . . . . . . . . . . . . . . . . . . . . . .
> She'll cut her throat at ten if she's mad at two.

"Amnesiac," in its expression of the poet's isolation and the ambivalence of wife toward husband, expands sexual conflict to include both husband and father:

> No use, no use, now begging Recognize!
> There is nothing to do with such a beautiful blank but smooth it.
> Name, house, car keys,
>
> The little toy wife—
> Erased, sigh, sigh. . . .
>
> Hugging his pillow
>
> Like the red-haired sister he never dared to touch,
> He dreams of a new one—
> Barren, the lot are barren!

And for the first time, the conclusion points in an inevitable direction, anticipating the Lethe of "Getting There": "O sister, mother, wife, / Sweet Lethe is my life. / I am never, never, never coming home!"[9]

"Mystic" also shows the abandonment of hope, discarding one by one possible sources of meaning or of spiritual or emotional sustenance:

> Once one has seen God, what is the remedy?
> Once one has been seized up
>
> Without a part left over—
> . . . . . . . . . . . . . . . . . . . . .
> What is the remedy?

The pill of the Communion tablet,
The walking beside still water? Memory?
. . . . . . . . . . . . . . . . . . . . . . . . . . . . . .
Is there no great love, only tenderness?
Does the sea

Remember the walker upon it?[10]

In other poems the split selves of spinster and strumpet are represented not as separate people but as separate, vying forces. "O love, O
celibate," cries the speaker of "Letter in November." The conflict may be
realized in a number of ways—in the poem's words directly, or in a close
relation between the poem's sound and sense, or in the poem's imagery.
It may be expressed even in puns; the speaker-victim of "Daddy" has
chosen a husband with "a love of the rack and the screw."

But no matter how it is rendered, the conflict involves the love and
hate of strumpet and celibate for one another, for their acts, and for their
chosen types of lovers. In its absolute impossibility of reconciliation in
life, the frustration requires death for its resolution, a death that is at
once actual and sexual, an end and a beginning. And this inevitable
death is not only accepted by the poet—it is desired. As the conflict
joins love with hate and end with beginning, it also joins love with
death. In "The Couriers," many familiar images connote death, while
the poet speaks its conjunction with love:

> Frost on a leaf, the immaculate
> Cauldron, talking and crackling
>
> A disturbance in mirrors,
> The sea shattering its grey one—
>
> Love, love, my season.

The tension between all of these forces, desires, and restraints is powerfully and excellently expressed in "Fever 103°." Here the speaker's words
express her inner conflict; though she has been in bed with her lover all
night, the strumpet has achieved only limited success: "Darling, all night /
I have been flickering, off, on, off, on. / The sheets grow heavy as a lecher's

kiss" and the spinster, who has been asking disturbing questions about purity, punishment, and adultery, has finally gained control: "I am too pure for you or anyone. / Your body / Hurts me as the world hurts God. I am a lantern—" But the control is of the mind only. Her new heat and passion are, in the words' meaning, the heat of religious fervor, of an "acetylene Virgin." But the poem's rhythms say that her heat and passion are intensely sexual; as the lines decrease in length, as the cadences become regular and then grow rhythmically faster and shorter, what we hear—not in words—is an incredible build toward orgasm:

> Does not my heat astound you. And my light.
> All by myself I am a huge camellia
> Glowing and coming and going, flush on flush.
>
> I think I am going up,
> I think I may rise—
> The beads of hot metal fly, and I, love, I
>
> Am a pure acetylene
> Virgin
> Attended by roses,
>
> By kisses, by cherubim,
> By whatever these pink things mean.
> Not you, nor him
>
> Not him, nor him
> (My selves dissolving, old whore petticoats)—
> To Paradise.

By simultaneously affirming purity and dramatizing orgasm, this climax both enacts the strumpet-spinster conflict and denies its very existence at the peak moment ("Virgin"). Here, sexual release is also release into death.

The conflict is complex and unresolvable. The despair it engendered in the earlier poems has now changed to anger or resignation, expressed in various moods. The desperate hope of "Mystic" is largely absent from

the final poems, and when the poet is not loudly, or mockingly, or defi-
antly decrying her fate, she is describing it in an empty, flat voice:

> This is the light of the mind, cold and planetary.
> . . . . . . . . . . . . . . . . . . . . . . . . . . . . . . . . . . .
> The moon is no door. It is a face in its own right,
> . . . . . . . . . . . . . . . . . . . . . . . . . . . . . . . . . . .
> With the O-gape of complete despair. I live here.
> . . . . . . . . . . . . . . . . . . . . . . . . . . . . . . . . . . .
> The yew tree points up. It has a Gothic shape.
> The eyes lift after it and find the moon.
> The moon is my mother. She is not sweet Mary.
> Her blue garments unloose small bats and owls.
> How I would like to believe in tenderness—
> . . . . . . . . . . . . . . . . . . . . . . . . . . . . . . . . . . .
> The moon sees nothing of this. She is bald and wild.
> And the message of the yew tree is blackness—blackness and
> silence.
>
> ("The Moon and the Yew Tree")

## The Rival

The complexity of this conflict deepens when another element is admitted to it. The poems' internal tension between resignation and resistance, despair and hope, rejection and approval, love and hate, fertility
and barrenness, life and death is amplified when we examine the "rival"
poems, some of which Plath intended for *Ariel* but which Hughes
deleted as too "personally aggressive." Plath's "The Rival" of July 1961
is oddly prophetic, for Plath was soon to have an actual rival for her husband's affection, a rivalry she finally lost when Hughes left her to live
with Assia Wevill. And Plath's discovery of the affair (while she and
Hughes lived in Devon) provides the occasion for much of the desperation, self-doubt, and anger expressed in her poetry from the summer of
1962 until her death.

   None of these poems appears in Hughes's *Ariel*; some were published
later in *Winter Trees*; others appeared first in *The Collected Poems*. "Words
heard, by accident, over the phone" is Plath's response to a phone call to

Ted from Assia. It may be Hughes's absence that makes Nicholas "fatherless" in "For a Fatherless Son." The speaker of "The Detective" is a Sylvia Plath–Sherlock Holmes character sniffing out "deceits" and finding the man's "smile" to be his "death weapon." "The Courage of Shutting-Up" reports the speaker's sense of grim "outrage" in the face of "accounts of bastardies. / Bastardies, usages, desertions and doubleness." "The secret is stamped on you," intones the speaker of "A Secret" in lines reminiscent of "Daddy" (written only two days later in October 1962), and that is "a difference between us." In "The Jailer," the speaker reflects on her captivity: "I am myself. That is not enough." "What have I eaten? / Lies and smiles." The "little toy wife" in "Amnesiac" is "Erased, sigh, sigh"; while the husband "dreams of a new one," the present wife declares "Sweet Lethe is my life." "The Fearful," echoing "Words heard, by accident, over the phone," refers to an actual call from Assia that Sylvia answered: "This woman on the telephone / Says she is a man, not a woman."

## Children

In spite of the prevalent anger, blankness, and despair in these late poems, however, there are among them several "baby" poems, addressed lovingly by the speaker to her child. For brief moments, perhaps, the mother's love may provide partial relief from the otherwise unrelieved world of nightmare. "You're" is an affectionate, droll poem, with wonderfully clever images. There, the baby is

> Clownlike, happiest on your hands,
> . . . . . . . . . . . . . . . . . . . . . . . . . . .
> Mute as a turnip from the Fourth
> Of July to All Fool's Day.
> O high-riser, my little loaf.
> . . . . . . . . . . . . . . . . . . . . . . . . . . .
> Jumpy as a Mexican bean.
> Right, like a well-done sum.
> A clean slate, with your own face on.

The child is innocent, new, unacquainted with pain; in "Child," similarly, his "clear eye is the one absolutely beautiful thing. / I want to fill it with colour and ducks." Too, "Morning Song" and "Balloons" and "For a Fatherless Son" are loving and whimsical musings of mother to baby. In these poems the child's "clear vowels rise like balloons"; he is a precious little bundle of time, a "fat gold watch" recently "set going" by "love"; his "smiles are found money."

Yet the imagery of disintegration and death invades even these poems. The baby of "You're" is "moon-skulled"; in "Child" he

> Should be grand and classical
>
> Not this troublous
> Wringing of hands, this dark
> Ceiling without a star.

The precious child of "Morning Song" is also a "New statue / In a drafty museum"; in "Balloons" he holds "a red / Shred in his little fist"; and the fatherless son "will be aware of an absence, presently, / Growing beside you like a tree, / A death tree, colour gone." There are dead babies in "Death & Co.," and the woman who is perfected by death in "Edge" holds her dead children at her breast.

And so the unmitigated conflict, "this dark thing" of "Elm," unbearably rages and bursts out in a single cry:

> I am inhabited by a cry.
> Nightly it flaps out
> Looking, with its hooks, for something to love.
>
> I am terrified by this dark thing
> That sleeps in me;
> . . . . . . . . . . . . . . . . .
> What is this, this face
> So murderous in its strangle of branches—?
>
> Its snaky acids kiss.
> It petrifies the will. These are the isolate, slow faults
> That kill, that kill, that kill.

## Formal Control

There is no letting up in these poems, no release whatever. The poet is indeed inhabited by her cry; her nightmare is real, and reality is the nightmare. And in informing it, much of the power derives from the controlling, but not taming, influence the poetic structure exerts upon the poet's outpourings. Not only do the breakdown of exterior-interior boundaries, the highly symbolic landscapes, and the particularized set of images require special control because of their wild, hallucinatory nature; they also provide control as they define the limits of a nightmarish world. In this poetry, well-established boundaries guide the turbulent stream and cause it to flow faster. Economy relates directly to intensity.

In this economizing, intensifying role, the poems' structures play an important part. Most of the poems in *Ariel* and *Winter Trees* differ from the earlier ones, as we have seen, by being more emphatic, more direct, simpler, and more linguistically natural. And the increase in excellence here is related in part to a decreasing concern on Plath's part with formal stanza and end-rhyme constructions.

One exception to this rule, however, demands attention. The only poem among the late ones with consistent end-rhyme and rhythmic regularity from beginning to end is "Daddy," a poem that suffers no loss of power from its apparently conventional structure. Its rhythm is anapestic trimeter with many irregularities; its end-rhyme, "oo," falls into no particular pattern but concludes a minimum of one line in every five-line stanza (with the exception of only 1 stanza out of 16 where it is not used at all) and a maximum of five lines. In these sounds and rhythms, "Daddy" has clear affinities with the nursery rhyme, a mode that provides, in this case, an obviously ironic structure. Indeed, in her adoption of this form, Plath has intentionally linked the nursery-rhyme world with the world of the poem to create a precariously balanced tension between the two. Furthermore, as A. Alvarez suggests, the nursery rhyme may have provided for Plath an essential "manic defence" against the insufferable.[11] Certainly, this is Plath's starkest confrontation with the "daddy" problem evident throughout her work; because the sense that drives this poem is perhaps more painful to her than any other, a real need may exist for the extra edge of control afforded by regular form. The rhythm is the rhythm of ritual, and the ritual is one both of death and of love. A. R. Jones observes that the poem's "main area of conflict" is the psyche of the persecuted speaker, with its final knowledge, from which she can escape only into death, that love expresses itself only in terms of violence and brutality.[12]

In spite of the regularity, then, this poem is not a misfit in *Ariel*; the form is anything but rigid, and the poem reveals the same line-to-line power seen in the other late poetry. The "Daddy" of the poem is the colossus; here as elsewhere he is both daddy and husband. And the work jauntily but terrifyingly synthesizes the poet's problem:

> You do not do, you do not do
> Any more, black shoe
> In which I have lived like a foot
> For thirty years, poor and white,
> Barely daring to breathe or Achoo.
> . . . . . . . . . . . . . . . . . . . . . . . . . .
> I was ten when they buried you.
> At twenty I tried to die
> And get back, back, back to you.
> I thought even the bones would do.
>
> But they pulled me out of the sack,
> And they stuck me together with glue.
> And then I knew what to do.
> I made a model of you,
> A man in black with a Meinkampf look
>
> And a love of the rack and the screw.
> And I said I do, I do.
> So daddy, I'm finally through.
> The black telephone's off at the root,
> The voices just can't worm through.
>
> If I've killed one man, I've killed two—
> The vampire who said he was you
> And drank my blood for a year,

> Seven years, if you want to know.
> Daddy, you can lie back now.
>
> There's a stake in your fat black heart
> And the villagers never liked you.
> They are dancing and stamping on you.
> They always knew it was you.
> Daddy, daddy, you bastard, I'm through.

The other, less regular poems in *Ariel* and *Winter Trees* are powerful for basically the same reasons "Daddy" is. Intensity resides in the emotion expressed, to be sure, but the poems are powerful because of the one-to-one relation between sense and structure. Aural texture is vivid and effective; Plath's experimentation with sound in the earlier works most certainly serves her well in these late ones. The tongue-twisting quality of such early poems as "Snakecharmer," "Sow," and "The Hermit at Outermost House" gives way, in the final poems, to the lightly appropriate sound patterns of such poems as "Daddy," or "Gigolo":

> Pocket watch, I tick well.
> The streets are lizardy crevices
> Sheer-sided, with holes where to hide.
> . . . . . . . . . . . . . . . . . . . . . . . . . . . . .
> Bright fish hooks, the smiles of women
> Gulp at my bulk
> And I, in my snazzy blacks
>
> Mill a litter of breasts like jellyfish.
> To nourish
> The cellos of moans I eat eggs—

Here, word sounds reinforce one another to intensify meaning; indeed, word sounds actually *provide* meaning so that the texture of the poem's language itself presents the experience being offered in the poem.

Even more striking than the sounds of individual words are the feeling and even the sound of motion the poetry projects through its line lengths and its distinct though often fragmentary rhythms. Again, the poet's ear-

lier experimentation with such stylized and demanding structures as the
villanelle and terza rima, her practice in writing strictly patterned stanzas
both long and short, serve her well in this late work. For the poems of
*Ariel* and *Winter Trees* conform not to an externally imposed pattern, but
rather to the pattern demanded by the poem's sense. Short lines, abrupt
enjambments, and jerking rhythms effectively convey the speaker's
clipped tones, laden with emotion and/or rage about to break the lines'
tight restrictions, in such poems as "Lady Lazarus" or "Purdah":

> Attendants!
> And at his next step
> I shall unloose
> I shall unloose—
> From the small jewelled
> Doll he guards like a heart—
>
> The lioness,
> The shriek in the bath,
> The cloak of holes.
>
> ("Purdah")

Longer lines, and easier rhythms, evoke also the speaker's emotional
condition, as in the drained cadences of a poem like "Contusion":

> Colour floods to the spot, dull purple.
> The rest of the body is all washed out,
> The colour of pearl.
> . . . . . . . . . . . . . . . . . . . . . . . . . . . . .
> The heart shuts,
> The sea slides back,
> The mirrors are sheeted.

Similar pacing can also inform the wistful, poignant expression of the
mother-to-child poems. In any case, rhythms, and line and stanza
length (and, indeed, the length of the poem itself) are determined by
sense; in the late poetry, structure and sense are joined inextricably. As

Stephen Spender has commented, "The length of the poem is decided by the duration of the poet's vision, which is far more serious to the poet than formal considerations" (Spender, 25).

Closely connected, of course, to this organic relation of sense with structure is the oral quality achieved in the late poems. They require, as Plath has remarked, to be read aloud. However various the cadences of *Ariel* and *Winter Trees* may be, they are the cadences of speech, the rhythms of a person talking. The poet has progressed from the often stilted rhythms of the early work, through the easier, more natural rhythms of *Crossing the Water*, to the appropriate and diverse rhythms of the last poems.

The voice play "Three Women" presents a fine example of this achievement. This "Poem for Three Voices" consists of a kind of triple dramatic monologue, offering in time sequence the experiences of three women before, during, and after miscarriage or childbirth. As such, it evinces not only Plath's achievement of verisimilitude in her characters' speech but also her shedding of the self-consciousness so apparent in the transitional work, so that she creates here believable and forceful dramatic situations.

The speakers of this dramatic voice poem are a wife, a secretary (also a wife), and an unmarried girl. The setting, as Plath directs, is "A Maternity Ward and round about." As the poem progresses, each character recollects the series of events that brought her there, and each, expressing her anticipations, fears, and thoughts, is clearly individual and compellingly credible. For example, the poem opens as the first voice (the wife) reflects upon her gravid condition:

> When I walk out, I am a great event.
> I do not have to think, or even rehearse.
> What happens in me will happen without attention.
> The pheasant stands on the hill;
> He is arranging his brown feathers.
> I cannot help smiling at what it is I know.
> Leaves and petals attend me. I am ready.

The second voice (the secretary) has miscarried her baby; she describes her reaction in terms that echo another of Plath's late poems, "The Moon and the Yew Tree":

There is the moon in the high window. It is over.
How winter fills my soul! And that chalk light
Laying its scales on the windows, the windows of empty offices,
Empty schoolrooms, empty churches. O so much emptiness!
There is this cessation. This terrible cessation of everything.
These bodies mounded around me now, these polar sleepers—
What blue, moony ray ices their dreams?

And the third voice (the girl) expresses her fear before giving birth:

And what if two lives leaked between my thighs?
I have seen the white clean chamber with its instruments.
It is a place of shrieks. It is not happy.
"This is where you will come when you are ready."
The night lights are flat red moons. They are dull with blood.
I am not ready for anything to happen.
I should have murdered this, that murders me.

As all three women speak, their voices are distinct and their diction
appropriate. Only the first voice, as we come to know it, could express
the mature calm of "I am ready"; only the second voice could utter the
sharp despair of "I am restless. Restless and useless. I, too, create
corpses." And only the girlish third voice, "not ready for anything to
happen," could pronounce the thought "I should have murdered this,
that murders me." As Douglas Cleverdon observes, "The emotional
experience" of the three women "is shaped by poetic discipline into the
most austere and monosyllabic forms. In radio, nothing can equal a
poet's visualizing imagination, dramatically expressed in clear and
speakable language."[13] And, in fact, nothing can equal such an achievement in poetry, either.

## Final Achievement

Clearly, then, Plath's uses of sound and structure, of rhythm and language, are imaginative, varied, and always appropriate in her final
poems; the lines quoted from these poems attest to this achievement
and to the control and economy realized thereby. The poet has truly
become a master of her form; the poems now are economical and appro-

priate in technique, powerful and yet controlled in expression, and incisive and original in conception. Two final, specific examples will underline the point.

The poem "Tulips" exemplifies one particular style Plath uses; its lines are long and relatively smooth, and its rhythm is fairly constant though not conventionally regular. Its stanzas are like paragraphs, each one exploring a new area of the main idea. And each "paragraph" is unified by a single image that relates to every other unifying image all of which, together, comprise the whole poetic statement. The poem moves by means of its subtly shifting images as several aspects of a single scene are called to attention. The effect is that of a very simple red and white kaleidoscope; the scene's components obtrude and recede, and the pattern changes as values are transferred from one object to another. The "I" of the poem is a postoperative patient still in the hospital, "learning peacefulness, lying by myself quietly / As the light lies on these white walls, . . . / I am nobody." Quietness is the mood of sense and rhythm with a few notable exceptions. Stanza two presents an eye image:

> They have propped my head between the pillow and the sheet-cuff
> Like an eye between two white lids that will not shut.
> Stupid pupil, it has to take everything in.

"Stupid pupil" in the midst of longer, smoother phrases offers significant, thematic contrast. And the manipulation of imagery is particularly evident if we compare stanza 2 with stanza 7, where the pupil, the patient's white, "cut-paper shadow" nonface, now lies between red borders instead of white, themselves eyes:

> Nobody watched me before, now I am watched.
> The tulips turn to me, and the window behind me
> Where once a day the light slowly widens and slowly thins,
> And I see myself, flat, ridiculous, a cut-paper shadow
> Between the eye of the sun and the eyes of the tulips.
> And I have no face, I have wanted to efface myself.
> The vivid tulips eat my oxygen.

The last line of this stanza introduces the red and white air imagery of the next stanza, and so forth. Notice, too, the similarity of the "cut-paper shadow" here to the "cut-paper people" of the transitional poem "Crossing the Water." Surely the contrast between the effectiveness of that image in "Tulips" and its impotency in the earlier poem is one more positive testament to Plath's poetic achievement in her final work.

"Tulips" moves by subjective association, like a dream, or a nightmare. But the poet never releases her control, whether writing in the "tulips" style or in the jagged style she employs more often in *Ariel* and *Winter Trees*. Of this latter technique, the poem "Lady Lazarus" offers a particularly vivid example. The sense of a nightmarish circus world found in the early poem "Circus in Three Rings" pervades "Lady Lazarus," but the greater intensity of the later poem derives from the shorter, choppy lines; the overlay of a biting, sardonic tone onto the defiant mood; and the shifting rhythmic patterns. The speaker is the poet herself, "the magician's girl who does not flinch" ("The Bee Meeting"), a sort of circus freak lady. She begins:

> I have done it again.
> One year in every ten
> I manage it—
>
> A sort of walking miracle,
> . . . . . . . . . . . . . . . . . .
> Peel off the napkin
> O my enemy.
> Do I terrify?—
>
> The nose, the eye pits, the full set of teeth?
> The sour breath
> Will vanish in a day.
> . . . . . . . . . . . . . . . . . .
> What a million filaments.
> The peanut-crunching crowd
> Shoves in to see
>
> Them unwrap me hand and foot—
> The big strip tease.
> Gentlemen, ladies,

> These are my hands
> My knees.
> I may be skin and bone,
>
> Nevertheless, I am the same, identical woman.

The poem jerks ahead through Lady Lazarus's hideous performance as the calloused circus performer makes her bitterly trenchant statement. And in determining the implications of that statement, a look at the Lazarus reference is instructive. One biblical Lazarus, the one we probably think of first in connection with Plath's poem, is the one who was raised from the dead, emerging from his grave (like the lady of the poem) "bound hand and foot with graveclothes: and his face was bound about with a napkin" (John 11:44). Notice how closely Plath uses the language of the biblical account. But there is another Lazarus as well, a beggar, "full of sores," which "the dogs came and licked." This beggar, Lazarus, is refused aid by a rich man, and when both men die, it is Lazarus and not the rich man who achieves heaven: "Remember," God says to the rich man, "that thou in thy lifetime receivedst thy good things, and likewise Lazarus evil things; but now he is comforted, and thou art tormented" (Luke 16:19–26). Beneath the defiant cadences of the poem, then, is both a plea for help and a damning indictment of the unwilling helper. Such a reading is certainly reinforced by the poem's familiar imagery of Jew and enemy. If Lady Lazarus—the poet herself, the Jew—is in torment now, her victimizers will suffer great torment later. As the poem continues, its rhythm suddenly becomes quite regular as Lady Lazarus shifts into a bitter mocking of her "act" and even of herself:

> Dying
> Is an art, like everything else.
> I do it exceptionally well.
>
> I do it so it feels like hell.
> I do it so it feels real.
> I guess you could say I've a call.

Then, from this point to the poem's close, the two rhythms interchange and mingle.

No further testament is needed to the power of this poetry or the skill of its author. Plath said once that the finest works of her favorite poets "seem born all-of-a-piece, not put together by hand"; [14] in the late poems of *Ariel* and *Winter Trees*, she too has achieved this style. In her last years, Plath disciplined her cry into a number of cogent, convincing poems in which all parts work perfectly together. She did indeed succeed in informing her "cries from the heart" and in ordering even the most terrifying of experiences; in this work, both poet and poem "melt to a shriek" that is at once utterly uncontrollable and finally controlled in the poem.

But does the poet's suicide finally negate the authenticity of the control these poems place upon their turbulent subjects? Or, indeed, are those very subjects validated in some way by the poet's death? Robert Lowell concludes that Plath's late poems "tell that life, even when disciplined, is simply not worth it." [15] But that is only part of what they tell. For the poems themselves do live on, surviving the death of their composer, as in fact all poems do. As the poet Anne Sexton, a friend of Plath's and herself a suicide, reminds us, "suicide is, after all, the opposite of the poem." [16] Finally, the poet's death must be regarded as an act that neither negates nor authenticates her work; death, after all, is not a poem. And these late poems, as Plath herself observed when speaking of great poetry, go "farther than the words of a classroom teacher or the prescriptions of a doctor; if they are very lucky, farther than a lifetime." [17]

## Chapter Eight
# God's Lioness

As soon as the major techniques and concerns of this utterly personal poetry emerge, one can see that it is essentially a contemporary restatement of the apocalyptic vision. Decked with surreal landscapes, mythological characters, scenes of World War II horrors, and glimpses of modern domestic life, the essential vision has been invoked and newly expressed to define the poet's present misery and her anticipation of triumphant release.

Because the late poems represent a culmination—in their subjects, images, and technical excellence—of Plath's whole poetic career, it is to these poems that we look for the most cogent statement of this vision. And in the same way that these final poems contain the major concerns of the whole canon (remember Ted Hughes's observation of "how faithfully her separate poems build up into one long poem"), the title poem of the volume *Ariel* presents the predominant concerns of the late work. "Ariel" is a compendium of the poetry; in it we find the sense of present oppression and despair, the belief in release from that oppression, and the notion of relentlessly, uncontrollably speeding ahead through an antipathetic landscape toward a goal at once destructive and ecstatic, an end and a beginning.

On an obvious level, "Ariel" describes a dawn ride that begins with the instant that the speaker, having mounted her horse, is poised for action ("Stasis in darkness"), continues as she gathers speed and intensity, and culminates as recognizable landscape dissolves and the speaker is violently propelled through air. Even in the poem's opening lines we recognize that this ride will have intangible as well as tangible qualities: "Stasis in darkness. / Then the substanceless blue / Pour of tor and distances."[1] Emerging from inaction, perhaps even specifically from a dark stable, into the light of early dawn, horse, rider, and landscape are all curiously "substanceless."

The effect of this "substanceless" quality is to permit a fusion of elements. Indeed, that fusion is the source both of the poem's strength and of its abstruseness; as A. Alvarez has pointed out, "the difficulty of this poem lies in separating one element from another. Yet that is also its

111

theme; the rider is one with the horse, the horse is one with the fur-
rowed earth, and the dew on the furrow is one with the rider."[2]

> God's lioness,
> How one we grow,
> Pivot of heels and knees!—The furrow
>
> Splits and passes, sister to
> The brown arc
> Of the neck I cannot catch. . . .

In the "pivot of heels and knees," horse and rider visually become "one,"
and we are told that furrow and horse are sisters.

It is at this point that we recognize the poem's thematic center. The
unity of rider with horse with furrow with dew, which Alvarez sees as
the poem's theme, encompasses only a part of the poem's elements. At
the center of this "substanceless" collection of ingredients is the word
*Ariel.* For one thing, Ariel is the name of Plath's horse, and as Ted
Hughes describes it, the experience that provides the simple, surface
sense of the poem is an actual one: "Ariel was the name of the horse on
which she went riding weekly. Long before, while she was a student at
Cambridge (England), she went riding with an American friend out
towards Grantchester. Her horse bolted, the stirrups fell off, and she
came all the way home to the stables, about two miles, at full gallop,
hanging around the horse's neck."[3] Included in this unity of elements,
then, is not just any rider, but the poet herself. Furthermore, it is
entirely possible that Plath, knowing that *Ariel* is the name of a kind of
Arabian gazelle, chose a name for her horse that suggested, among
other things, the gazelle's swiftness.

The various Ariels from literature are also germane to the sense of this
poem and of Plath's whole canon. Of principal importance is Shakespeare's Ariel, the tricksy spirit of *The Tempest*; because all things are fused
in Plath's poem, because horse and earth and poet are one, then the spirit
Ariel joins also in this unity. Several of his characteristics are relevant
here; for one thing, he is the poet and singer who creates spells with his
song. Furthermore, Shakespeare's Ariel, like the rebel angel of Milton's
*Paradise Lost* and Belinda's guardian in Pope's *The Rape of the Lock*, is
androgynous, capable of changing sex and shape at will. And so Plath, as
Ariel, can be variously Lady Lazarus, an elm tree, a man applying for a

wife, a mother, a Jew, a gigolo. Finally, and perhaps most important, Shakespeare's Ariel is captive, held in servitude by his master Prospero:

ARIEL:    Is there more toil? Since thou dost give me pains,
            Let me remember thee what thou has promis'd.
            Which is not yet perform'd me.
PROSPERO:  How now! Moody?
            What is't thou canst demand?
ARIEL:    My liberty.
PROSPERO:  Before the time be out! No more! . . .
            Thou shalt be as free
            As mountain winds; but then exactly do
            All points of my command.
ARIEL:    To the syllable.[4]

And significantly, one short poem in *Ariel*, "The Hanging Man," alludes directly to this Ariel of *The Tempest*:

By the roots of my hair some god got hold of me.
I sizzled in his blue volts like a desert prophet.

The nights snapped out of sight like a lizard's eyelid:
A world of bald white days in a shadeless socket.

A vulturous boredom pinned me in this tree.
If he were I, he would do what I did.[5]

    This sense of present oppression and anticipation of release and freedom is thematically central to Plath's poetry. It may be expressed, for example, as attainment of "perfection," as in "Edge," where the dead woman "is perfected," or in "The Munich Mannequins" ("Perfection is terrible, it cannot have children"), or in "Three Women," where the secretary's aborted fetus is

the unborn one that loved its perfections,
The face of the dead one that could only be perfect
In its easy peace, could only keep holy so.[6]

Or it may appear as the queen bee's triumphant and phoenixlike flight from those who would retain and kill her, or as suicidal escape from the murderous influence of daddy and husband.

Moreover, this theme of oppression and release is invoked in yet another way, and the reference is ultimately significant not only to the poem "Ariel" but to Plath's entire vision. In "Purdah," the poet characterizes that part of herself that rages for release and thirsts for destruction (and self-destruction), as a "lioness":

> I shall unloose—
> From the small jewelled
> Doll he guards like a heart—
>
> The lioness,
> The shriek in the bath,
> The cloak of holes.[7]

And in "Ariel," she becomes the lioness totally: "God's lioness, / How one we grow." Significantly, the Greek word *Ariel*, from the Hebrew word *Ariel*, means "lioness of God." In the Bible it is a designation given by Isaiah to the city of Jerusalem, a city that is presently the object of God's wrath and condemned to tribulation but which is promised deliverance in the apocalypse:

Woe to Ariel, to Ariel, the city where David dwelt! add ye year to year; let them kill sacrifices.

Yet I will distress Ariel, and there shall be heaviness and sorrow: and it shall be unto me as Ariel.

And I will camp against thee round about, and will lay seige against thee with a mount, and I will raise forts against thee. . . .

Moreover the multitude of thy strangers shall be like small dust, and the multitude of the terrible ones shall be as chaff that passeth away: yea, it shall be at an instant suddenly.

Thou shalt be visited of the Lord of hosts with thunder, and with earthquake, and great noise, with storm and tempest, and the flame of devouring fire.

And the multitude of all the nations that fight against Ariel, even all that fight against her and her munition, and that distress her, shall be as a dream of a night vision.

(Isaiah 29:1–3, 5–7)

Ariel, then, is poet, rider, and horse; she is a swift, indomitable presence galloping unflinchingly ahead; and she is an androgynous spirit assuming the form of anything or anyone who is oppressed and yearning for freedom. She is God's lioness. Ariel is also a specific poem and a volume of poetry, and in its unity of elements Ariel becomes also a metaphor for the poet's vision.

The poem's lines continue to display and define specific aspects of that vision:

> Nigger-eye
> Berries cast dark
> Hooks—

> Black sweet blood mouthfuls,
> Shadows.

The poet's present condition is indeed one of captivity and suffering; hooks, blackness, and darkness are familiar images Plath uses elsewhere to express this. But inherent in the present misery is the expectation of its end. The suffering is merely prerequisite to release; the "black, blood mouthfuls" are "sweet."

This release has been anticipated from the poem's beginning, from the horse's first step into the "substanceless" landscape. All the while, forward motion has been intensifying; the powerful gallop is uncontrollable now, and Ariel seems to burst through the limits of earthly reality into a new, even more "substanceless" order:

> Something else

> Hauls me through air—
> Thighs, hair;
> Flakes from my heels.

> White
> Godiva, I unpeel—
> Dead hands, dead stringencies.
>
> And now I
> Foam to wheat, a glitter of seas.
> The child's cry
>
> Melts in the wall.

This is the purifying process of "Fever 103°" and "Tulips," the unpeeling of "Lady Lazarus" and "Getting There." The "stringencies" are "dead"; the hooks are at last powerless to detain her. The goal of this ride is in sight; the "glitter" here, and the "dew" of the following lines, are death, the dead bell's companion in "Death & Co.," the glitter in "Berck-Plage," "Gigolo," and "Purdah," the shimmering veil to be "let down" in "A Birthday Present," the "dewdrop" at the end of the journey in "Getting There." Even the very kind of motion assumes death as the terminal. In "Years," the poet confesses that

> What I love is
> The piston in motion—
> My soul dies before it.
> And the hooves of the horses,
> Their merciless churn.[8]

And we find the galloping hooves of "Ariel" in "Sheep in Fog" or "Elm," the relentless motion of the piston in the Nazi train of "Getting There" or in the train on which the secretary of "Three Women," during her miscarriage, imagines herself:

> I am dying as I sit. I lose a dimension.
> Trains roar in my ears, departures, departures!
> The silver track of time empties into the distance,
> The white sky empties of its promise, like a cup.[9]

The poem's closing lines complete the flight and provide release. Here, recognizable landscape is completely abandoned; surroundings

seem more emotional than physical. As the move toward a pure substanceless state is achieved, the fused identities of horse and rider
become an "arrow":

> And I
> Am the arrow,
>
> The dew that flies
> Suicidal, at one with the drive
> Into the red
>
> Eye, the cauldron of morning.

In these last lines one final element is aurally admitted into the unity
that has been expanding through the poem. We see here that "I," which
represents the oneness as it exists at this point, remains "at one with the
drive." And merging with it is the "Eye," which is for one thing the
bull's-eye, the target, the goal and end of this journey through present
misery and tribulation. But it is also the veil that is the last barrier to
apocalyptic triumph. It is both the redness of death and red morning
sun, the light of a new day, of rebirth.

From its opening lines, then, the poem has proceeded inexorably
toward this final breakthrough, so that the closing lines achieve both an
ultimate shedding of tangibility and a complete unity of elements. There
is also a rhythmic culmination in these lines. As we have previously
noticed, the horse's gallop has been growing faster and more uncontrollable through the poem. And here, at the end, a kind of rhythmic climax
is reached at exactly the moment that the last veil is rent. One way to
trace this increase in intensity is by means of the poem's verbs; at first the
earth only "splits and passes" the rider, but as speed increases she is
"haul[ed] through air," she "Foam[s]," and finally she is "the arrow" that
"flies / Suicidal." The intensification of movement is traceable also in the
poem's rhythms; the rhythms of "Ariel" are clearly sexual, much like the
rhythms of "Fever 103°." Accordingly, the early cadences of the poem,
where the speaker remains earthbound, are relatively calm; a shift occurs
when she breaks from earth and "Something else hauls me through air."
From this point on, the lines grow shorter and the rhythms faster,
increasing in tension toward the climactic "Eye." Release and resolution,
"the cauldron of morning," follow immediately to end the poem.

This special release is characteristic not only of this poem but also of most of the other poems in *Ariel* and *Winter Trees* and indeed throughout Plath's canon. In one way or another, conveyed variously by certain images or by orgasmic rhythms, Plath expresses repeatedly the notions of present suffering and servitude, of violent and/or ecstatic death, and of triumph and new life as an immediate condition of that death. She is God's lioness; her vision is apocalyptic.

This is not to say, however, that she can forecast the exact nature of the new order or describe for us the particulars of the millennium. Of this her poetry gives only clues. What she does, instead, is descry present danger and woe, call attention to the tribulation of Jerusalem. She "warns," says Stephen Spender, which is "all a poet can do today." She manages to "turn our horrors and our achievements into the same witches' brew" until we are made to see that "a spaceman promenading in space is not too distant a relation from a man in a concentration camp, and that everything is a symptom of the same holocaust" (Spender, 26). Yet in the very act of warning she anticipates the cataclysmic end of this present holocaust, and in so doing she becomes a herald of the apocalypse. David's city may presently be "visited . . . with thunder, and with earthquake, and great noise, with storm and tempest, and the flame of devouring fire," but it looks forward also to the time when "the multitude of all the nations that fight against Ariel, . . . and all that distress her, shall be as a dream of a night vision" (Isaiah 29:6–7).

In Plath's poems that night vision, the nightmare, assumes several identities. The tribulation of Ariel may appear as the anguish of Oedipus, the torture of the victimized Jew, the agony of ambivalent sexual attitudes, the grief of rejection, or the mother's poignant fear for her child. But whatever guise it assumes, the world of Ariel is the world of the nightmare in substance as well as in the surreal quality of its expression.

Apocalyptic release from the holocaust is both suicidal and ecstatic, and it always involves an act of purification, either religious, or fiery, or both. It is conveyed in several ways, one of which is by means of the phoenix symbol. In these late poems, the mention of ash, or the color red, or fire, or upward flight, dominate the closing lines, as, for example, in "Ariel": "Suicidal, at one with the drive / Into the red / Eye, the cauldron of morning"; or "Lady Lazarus": "Out of the ash / I rise with my red hair"[10]; or "Stings":

> Now she is flying
> More terrible than she ever was, red

> Scar in the sky, red comet
> Over the engine that killed her—[11]

or "Fever 103°":

> I think I am going up,
> I think I may rise—
> The beads of hot metal fly, and I, love, I
>
> Am a pure acetylene
> Virgin
> Attended by roses,
>
> . . . . . . . . . . . . . .
> To Paradise.[12]

In its use of the "Virgin," "Fever 103°" combines with the phoenix symbol another of the means Plath uses to express release or rebirth. The resurrected self may also be a totally pure, virginal woman. We see this also, for example, in "A Birthday Present":

> Is this the one for the annunciation?
> . . . . . . . . . . . . . . . . . . . . . . . . . . . . . . . . . . . . . . . . .
> There would be nobility then, there would be a birthday.
> And the knife not carve, but enter
>
> Pure and clean as the cry of a baby,
> And the universe slide from my side.[13]

And in "Childless Woman": "This body, / This ivory, / Godly as a child's shriek."[14]

In their mention of the baby, "A Birthday Present" and "Childless Woman" show still another means Plath uses to convey the theme of release. As we saw in the transitional poem "Face-Lift," the poem's speaker may anticipate literal rebirth, may be "Mother to myself." In that case, the death day becomes also the birth day, and the birth is achieved in specific ways. In "A Birthday Present" the birth is Eve-like, "from my side." In "Getting There," the speaker can "Step to you from the black car of Lethe, / Pure as a baby." In "Mary's Song" it is the baby itself who faces death and sacramental resurrection ("O golden child the world will kill and eat"). The wife in "Three Women" expresses a similar attitude; about to give birth, she is "like a Mary." She is herself "sacrificial," but later fears for her baby boy, "swaddled in white bands." And in "Brasilia," the baby is "a nail / Driven, driven in" by "you who eat / People like light rays." In these poems, as in "Nick and the Candlestick," the baby, symbol of hope and new life for the mother, must himself suffer his present existence and anticipate apocalyptic release:

> The pain
> You wake to is not yours.
> . . . . . . . . . . . . . . . . . . .
> You are the one
> Solid the spaces lean on, envious.
> You are the baby in the barn.[15]

Finally, the notion of death as a new beginning may be expressed in nuptial terms. In these poems, death day is not birth day but wedding day, as for example in "Little Fugue": "I survive the while, / Arranging my morning. . . . / The clouds are a marriage dress, of that pallor;"[16] or in "Purdah," in which the speaker who glitters like jade and "gleams like a mirror" awaits the bridegroom, "Lord of the mirrors," disturber of veils; or "Winter Trees," with its "series of weddings"; or in "Berck-Plage":

> A wedding-cake face in a paper frill.
> How superior he is now.
> . . . . . . . . . . . . . . . . . . . . . . . . . . . . . .
> And the bride flowers expend a freshness,
>
> And the soul is a bride
> In a still place, and the groom is red and forgetful, he is featureless.[17]

Such a metaphor is exactly appropriate in an apocalyptic vision such as Plath's. In the Bible, marriage with the bridegroom Christ is an apocalyptic act for which all must prepare and wait, as expressed, for instance, in the parable of the 10 virgins, where the 5 wise virgins, who remained watchful, "went in with him to the marriage": "Watch therefore, for ye know neither the day nor the hour wherein the Son of man cometh" (Matthew 25:1–13). Furthermore, in the Revelation of Saint John, this apocalyptic marriage includes Ariel specifically: "And I John saw the holy city, new Jerusalem, coming down from God out of heaven, prepared as a bride adorned for her husband" (Revelation 21:2). And it takes place to begin the millennium: "And the Spirit and the bride say, Come. And let him that heareth say, Come. And let him that is athirst come. And whosoever will, let him take the water of life freely" (Revelation 22:17).

Death is life, then, in Plath's vision, and earthly life is merely a prerequisite for death, often even a preparatory series of small deaths. As Robert Scholes observes, Plath's "works do not only come to us posthumously. They were written posthumously. Between suicides."[18] As she anticipates variously her triumphal resurrection, her rebirth into a new and wholly pure form, and her marriage, the poet is indeed Ariel, God's lioness.

# Chapter Nine

# The Life of the Work:
# Directions in Plath Scholarship

In contemplating and judging Plath's work, one may be keenly tempted to turn from an examination of the "posthumous" writing itself toward an analysis of the person who wrote it. Plath's poetry celebrates death, and we know that death is exactly and deliberately what the poet chose. Such knowledge, as in the case of any writer who has taken her or his own life, is difficult for readers to dismiss or ignore, for the writer's suicide informs and elucidates her words as we read them. We undergo a similar experience and feel a similar curiosity, for instance, when we study the poems of Anne Sexton or John Berryman. If we are to see the work of any such writer clearly, however, we must realize that the author's death finally neither negates nor authenticates the work, for the poems do not die with the poet. Yet, if Plath's art is not validated by her suicide, we may feel that the one appears to render the other more forthright, more genuine. She did what she said she would do.

Many readers want to know why she did it. Was her suicide a ploy for attention or a desperate cry for help, as some have suggested—even an act at which she intended to fail, as she had failed previously? Or did she mean to succeed, as others argue? Was her suicide the ultimate act of denial by a person to whom life was onerous and impossible—perhaps, specifically, an act of female sacrifice in a male-dominated, victimizing world? Was Plath deranged, the tortured prey of clinical depression that finally defeated her? Was she lonely, exhausted, ill, angry, or in thrall to Ted Hughes? Was her act a uniquely contemporary gesture, a horribly logical result of the kinds of imaginative risks vulnerable artists in our nihilistic modern society are forced to take?

These are the kinds of questions that have dominated Plath scholarship since the poet's death in 1963. While Plath lived, her work attracted little critical notice; after her suicide, her life, death, and work almost instantly became subjects of intense scrutiny. Over the intervening years, the character of that investigation has evolved from personal memoir to scholarly biography, from psychological analysis to critical investigation and appraisal, as time has begun to wear away the sharp edge of a poet's suicide and as Plath's estate has gradually released primary materials for publication or for study. Most of Plath's publications (and those that receive the most critical acclaim) have been posthumous, beginning with *Ariel* in 1965 and *The Bell Jar* (under Plath's own name) in 1967; continuing with *Crossing the Water* and *Winter Trees* in 1971, *Letters Home* in 1975, and *Johnny Panic and the Bible of Dreams* in 1977; and culminating with *The Collected Poems* in 1981, Smith College's acquisition of Plath's papers (including unpublished manuscripts) in the same year, and *The Journals* in 1982.

In a little more than two decades, biographies of Plath have contributed vigorously to Plath scholarship. Biographers have had progressively more material to work with (depending in part upon the extent and nature of the estate's cooperation in their work), augmenting the opportunity for informed and scholarly discussion. Their hypotheses and conclusions vary as widely as do their assessments of Plath's creative work and life: Edward Butscher (1976) dismisses Plath as a "bitch goddess." Linda Wagner-Martin (1987) regards Plath as a victim of the extremes of her own personality and, to some degree, of her husband's domination. Anne Stevenson (1989) aims to correct Wagner-Martin's view by attributing full blame to Plath herself, stressing Plath's "huge mood swings," her "manic violence," and her "paranoia." Ronald Hayman (1991) attributes Plath's suicide to "the triple convergence of the deep-seated death drive, the demoralizing circumstances in which she was living, and the effects of the [antidepressive] drugs" and argues that "in so far as her suicide was an act of aggression, it was aimed against [her husband, Ted Hughes] and his new lover, Assia Wevill." Paul Alexander (1991), who portrays Plath as a clinically depressed victim of her past and of her husband, also sees Hughes as the primary villain of Plath's story.

Plath criticism has benefited as well from the periodic appearance of poetry, fiction, letters, and journals in the years since the poet's death, probing and debating such issues as confessionalism, feminism, and biographical influence in Plath's work. As the number of available primary materials has increased, critical studies have multiplied. Essay collections can provide one measure of this growth: Charles Newman's pioneering *The Art of Sylvia Plath* was published in 1979, followed by Edward Butscher's *Sylvia Plath: The Woman and the Work* (1979), Linda W. Wagner's *Critical Essays on Sylvia Plath* (1984), and Paul Alexander's *Ariel Ascending* (1985). Within the past two decades, the appearance of two books has infused Plath studies with new energy: *Johnny Panic and the Bible of Dreams* (the first and only short story collection, although most stories had seen earlier, separate publication) and, especially, *The Collected Poems*, with its chronological arrangement and its revelations about the discrepancies between the order and contents of the published *Ariel* and Plath's careful intentions for the volume.

## Confession

Those who perceive Plath's suicide as a uniquely contemporary gesture are also, generally, those who see her as a member of poetry's confessional movement. Such a position does offer an explanation of suicide in terms we can discuss with some assurance, for it removes the act from the personal, private realm where we must deal with subjective or speculative materials and places it in a more accessible context. If Plath can accurately be considered a confessional poet, she is in the company of other well-known writers also subject to periodic breakdown and in some instances suicide—Hart Crane, Robert Lowell, John Berryman, Anne Sexton. Such similarity is not coincidental, for the writer of confession risks extreme distress. The confessional poet is one who, as the name implies, writes what appears to be personal confession, using the self as the center of investigation and offering what seem to be supremely private revelations. But the confessional poet, in the specific and contemporary sense, is more than that; he or she is, as the poet M. L. Rosenthal has observed, one whose work is "highly charged" and who makes of the private psychological vulnerability at the poem's center a cultural symbol, an "embodiment of . . . civilization."[1]

If the "confessional" label appears to suit Plath's writing, however, we should note that critics disagree not only about her membership in that school but about the meaning and value of "confession" as a poetic mode. Linda W. Wagner, for instance, observes that even though "critics writing as recently as the 1980s echoed [Rosenthal's] convenient term 'confessional' " with regard to Plath and others, "by the end of the 1970s the term had become almost completely pejorative."[2] Those who use the term pejoratively generally view confessional writing as self-indulgence, an isolated and solitary affair that does not locate itself in a larger cultural context. Thus, for example, Helen Vendler argues that Plath's "refusal to generalize . . . beyond her own case" prevented her from speaking "about the human condition" and "from seeing herself as one of many," so that "the resistance of experience to meaning"[3] contributed to her suicidal despair. Others take a similar position about confessionalism but reach a different conclusion about Plath. Reviewer Laurence Lerner, for instance, suggests that what readers identify as Plath's "confessional poetry" are "the great, frenetic outbursts which have become so famous." But, he argues, even Plath's late poems are not "confessional," which he equates with "artless," because they have "the true control of art."[4] And critic Stanley Plumly contends that "whatever 'confessional' means to the poetry to which it is too often ill-ascribed, it is first of all a kind of journalism, a reductive label . . . [that] would turn poetry into the prose of therapy." Because Plath's work "is a transformation, not an imitation," Plath should be considered not a confessional but a symbolist poet.[5]

Is Plath's poetry "confessional" because it offers only pure expression of anguish or derangement? Or is it confessional because it moves *beyond* anguish to prophecy and transmutes derangement into myth? Or is it *not* confessional because it transcends its anguish? Is another label, or any label at all, more appropriate? Plath's poetry is also called structuralist, mythic, linguistic, journalistic, romantic. Clearly, some difficulty lies in how one defines the term "confessional" in the first place. If we assign the term empirically and historically, rejecting the pejorative and observing the work of other confessional writers (Crane, Lowell, Sexton, Berryman), we shall include Plath in their number and reaffirm Rosenthal's definition, for most critics agree upon the contemporary, cultural significance of these poets' immediate, personal revelations. As they dare to explore the dark and obscure realms of consciousness, such poets expose themselves to grave emotional and psychological danger— as, for example, Plath does in her establishment of a metaphorical relationship between the quality of modern individual existence and such contemporary horrors as the atomic holocaust and the concentration camp. Plath's suicide, says Rosenthal, "is part of the imaginative risk"[6] that contemporary artists must take.

## Feminism

Feminist approaches also characterize Plath scholarship; Plath's achieved senses of victimization and entrapment, her rage, her declarations of independence, and her suicide are among the qualities that invite such readings of her poetry and fiction. And although Plath's attitudes as expressed in most of her work do indeed seem congruent with feminism, we should note the historical context of that work: *The Colossus* was pub-

lished in 1960; Plath died in 1963, the same year *The Bell Jar* was published; *Ariel* saw publication in 1965, the first of several volumes and
collections to be published posthumously. Betty Friedan's pioneering
*The Feminine Mystique* was published in 1963, the year of Plath's death,
and Mary Ellmann's *Thinking about Women* came out in 1968.
Critic Annette Kolodny offers a similar reminder:

> Had anyone had the prescience, in 1969, to pose the question of defining
> a "feminist" literary criticism, she might have been told, in the wake of
> Mary Ellmann's *Thinking About Women*, that it involved exposing the sex-
> ual stereotyping of women in both our literature and our literary criti-
> cism. . . . What could not have been anticipated in 1969, however, was
> the catalyzing force of an ideology that, for many of us, helped to bridge
> the gap between the world as we found it and the world as we wanted it
> to be.[7]

By this measure, Plath should surely be considered a feminist pioneer,
even though she wrote perhaps a decade too early to benefit from and
contribute to the movement. Pamela Annas agrees, pointing out that
Plath's "sense of entrapment, her sense that her choices are profoundly
limited, is directly connected to the particular time and place in which
she wrote her poetry," so that her "recurring metaphors of fragmenta-
tion and reification . . . are socially and historically based," particularly
in her late poem "The Applicant," which is "explicitly a portrait of marriage in contemporary Western culture."[8] Further, poet and critic Alicia
Ostriker emphasizes Plath's innovating feminist qualities:

> To my first encounter with Plath I date the initial stirrings of a realization
> . . . that [to live to be a hundred] will require, for me, reconciliation with
> a self that wants to kill or die. . . . It is an understanding I share with
> many other women, taught by Plath to recognise the underside of our
> womanly propriety. At the same moment as we are pulling ourselves
> from martyrdom's shadows to some sort of daylight, we honor her for
> being among the first to run a flashlight over the cave walls.[9]

Plath is surely involved in "exposing the sexual stereotyping of
women" and in recognizing "the underside of our womanly propriety."
Yet, a woman of her time, she seems to have been divided between
acculturation and instinct, paying lip service to contemporary values
and expressing what we may now call her feminism in unguarded (or
inspired) moments. In her marriage, she chose the role of domestic sub-

missiveness while placing the success of her husband's career above her own. She seems to have performed her duties as housewife conscientiously and well; she was a good cook, a thorough housekeeper, and a devoted mother. Susan R. Van Dyne, in her essay " 'More Terrible Than She Ever Was,' " argues for a crucial ambivalence in Plath's poetic and biological creativity, concluding that "whether consciously or intuitively, Plath . . . discover[ed] in the autumn of 1962 that her analogies [between writing poems and having babies] were false" and that "the coming of babies might have blocked her access to her creative powers."[10] It may also be true that a significant motivating factor in Plath's conjugal submission and domestic energy was her perfectionist tendency, the habit established early in her life of devoting her full energies to performing any task set before her. And it is even likely that her freedom to set priorities for her marriage was limited by her background and conditioning, specifically by the example and influence of her mother. Yet, as the critic Mary Lynn Broe observes, "Plath enlarges the definition of motherhood from one of passivity to an active transforming power" and dramatizes the formation of female personality as "that complex process of interplay between the history a woman inherits and the clear articulation of her developing consciousness."[11]

Surely Plath does explore vividly the "underside of our womanly propriety," the "self that wants to kill or die," for there is in her work a rage against men and a hatred of their oppressive power. As we have seen in *Ariel*, for instance, woman is man's prey, tormented beyond endurance by what she perceives as his impossible demands or reduced to the role of lifeless puppet by his destructive expectations. Even a partial survey of the *Ariel* poems underscores the point. In "The Applicant," the woman being offered as a wife is totally dehumanized, a "living doll," an "it" reduced to pure function: "It can sew, it can cook, / It can talk, talk, talk." In "The Rival," where the poem's very title may define the female–male relationship, the man is "beautiful, but annihilating." The speaker of "Lady Lazarus" is, in one of her guises, similar to the "living doll" of "The Applicant"; she is a circus freak lady performing her act, "the big strip tease." Under the napkin she is really a corpse that can "terrify" her audience by revealing "the nose, the eye pits, the full set of teeth," but she is nevertheless forced to conclude her act by playing the "smiling woman." In this poem, all male figures are the adversary; whether they are "Herr Doktor," the Nazi victimizer, or "Herr God," or "Herr Lucifer," they are all one "Herr Enemy." But in this poem the woman-victim also warns of her revenge: "Beware . . . I eat men like air." The terrible Nazi figure appears often in Plath's poetry; the Jew is his prey, and the woman thus assumes that role. In "Daddy," this "man in black with a Meinkampf look" is husband as well as father, a "bastard" whom the woman has had to kill. But the woman has not found release in her oppressor's death; inextricably bound to her captor, she has been forced to "[try] to die" to "get back" to him.

The materials and the texture of male oppression are vividly rendered in Plath's work, in her prose as well as in her poetry. Esther Greenwood of *The Bell Jar* may be seen, to a point, as the quintessential victim of a male-dominated society. Her confusion and breakdown result from her inability to integrate the conventional wisdom that has been externally imposed upon her with her basic personal instincts. Those people like Mrs. Willard and her mother who have thoroughly conditioned her sexual expectations are the most unliberated of women; Esther's role options, as she has learned them from women like these, are singularly unappealing. Esther can see no satisfactory self-fulfillment in female subservience and domestic submission; yet, because she has lacked a liberated role model and is too insecure to forge one for herself, she is cornered into increasing immobility. The female Dr. Nolan finally offers Esther the example and the help she needs to build a new, liberated personality and the strength to deal with the guilt that accompanies her discarding of the mother–Mrs. Willard norms. Esther's eventual marriage seems to represent her successful liberation; we are encouraged to assume that matrimony and motherhood, once her nemesis, no longer hinder her emancipated self-fulfillment. Yet this conclusion is not certain; it may be that Esther's marriage (implied but not realized in the novel) represents not success but failure to liberate herself. For Esther, marriage may herald the redescent of her stifling bell jar.     .

The attitude toward men that emerges from Plath's writing is one of love and hate intermixed; the destruction of her male oppressors requires also the destruction of herself. The only way for the speaker of her poems to deny the male victimizer, the only way not to be a victim, is to reject or destroy him altogether. But in so doing—in refusing, for example, to be the "Applicant's" "living doll"—she places herself in an equally impossible position, victimizing herself. For she is now condemned to an equally hateful existence of solitariness, chastity, and loneliness. As she says in "Elm," love may be terrifying and murderous; it kills; but she is also, as she recoils, "Inhabited by a cry" that looks "for something to love." In "Fever 103°" the "low smokes" of love and passion "roll" from her "like Isadora's scarves," and, like those scarves, they may kill her. "O love, O celibate," exclaims the speaker of "Letter in November"; she walks through a golden landscape where all the golds are "mouths of Thermopylae," gates so well defended that the enemy love has no chance to enter. Death and love go together. The need for love inevitably leads to figurative or actual death. Or, like Elizabeth Minton and the speaker of "Daddy," the woman must join her murdered lover-oppressor in death.

Whatever her priorities and conscious choices may have been, Plath did seek self-realization in ways available to her. She rebelled from time to time; we know from her letters and journals that she sometimes feared, or later resented, the restrictions of a wifely role. "Some pale, hueless flicker of sensitivity is in me," she wrote in her journal in 1951. "God, must I lose it in cooking scrambled eggs for a man . . . hearing about life at second hand?" (*J*, 33). She felt ambivalent about conventional gender roles. As early as 1950, she penned a line in her journal that she would later use in *The Bell Jar*: "Perry [Norton] said today that his mother said, 'Girls look for infinite security; boys look for a mate. . . .' I am at odds. I dislike being a girl, because as such I must come to realize that I cannot be a man . . . [and] I must pour my energies through the direction and force of my mate" (*J*, 23). She regretted that infant care and domestic duty left her little time to write, and she was bothered that she had no close personal friend. Perhaps the most significant measure of Plath's dissatisfaction with her conjugal situation was one of her responses to its collapse. After her separation from her husband, even though she had to continue keeping house and caring for her children, she began to write poems daily, urgently—as she said, as if domesticity had choked her. Plath was surely at this time at the edge of conscious feminist awareness; she might, had she lived longer, have been able to build from the wreckage of her marriage a self-reliant, clearly feminist point of view. But this is conjecture; she did not.

## The Two *Ariels*

With the 1981 publication of *The Collected Poems* came the astonishing news that Plath had carefully selected and planned *Ariel* for publication after her death and that the *Ariel* that readers and critics had studied for 16 years was not that volume. In his comments through the years on Plath's work, Ted Hughes had both hinted at and obfuscated this situation, remarking in "Notes on the Chronological Order of Sylvia Plath's Poems" that "Tulips," "Morning Song," and "Little Fugue" were "three that she selected for *Ariel*"[12] and commenting in his "Note" to the volume *Winter Trees* that "the poems in this volume are all out of the batch from which the *Ariel* poems were more or less arbitrarily chosen."[13] As the publication of *The Collected Poems* revealed, however, Plath had not chosen her *Ariel* "arbitrarily" but had carefully "selected" not three but all of the poems for her volume. In his introduction to *The Collected Poems*, Hughes discloses that the 1965 *Ariel* "was a somewhat different volume from the one [Plath] had planned. . . . It omitted some of the more personally aggressive poems from 1962" and "introduc[ed] her late work more cautiously" (*CP*, 15). And in his notes to *The Collected Poems*, Hughes lists the contents of "Sylvia Plath's own prepared collection of poems, titled *Ariel*" (*CP*, 295).

Responding to this information, scholars have been engaged in comparing the 1965 *Ariel* with the volume Plath intended, assessing the character of each, examining thematic arrangements, pondering Plath's reasons for selecting and arranging the poems as she did, and speculating about Hughes's reasons for defying Plath's intentions. Marjorie Perloff, for example, points out that "what Ted Hughes doesn't say [in his explanation quoted in the last paragraph] is that 'the more personally aggressive poems from 1962' he chose to omit were those that expressed, most directly and brutally, Plath's anger, bitterness, and despair over his desertion of her for another woman."[14] In her essay "The Two *Ariels*: The (Re)Making of the Sylvia Plath Canon," Perloff describes the differences between what she calls "*Ariel 1*" ("Plath's *Ariel*") and "*Ariel 2*" ("Hughes's construction of *Ariel*"), concluding that although Hughes's volume ends in a despair "beyond rage" that "implies that Plath's suicide was inevitable" and "was brought on, not by her actual circumstances but by her . . . seemingly incurable schizophrenia," Plath's *Ariel* "ends on a note of hope." As Perloff demonstrates, "Plath's arrangement emphasizes not death but struggle and revenge, the outrage that follows the recognition that the beloved is also the betrayer."[15]

Other critics comment as well on the importance of the thematic shift between the 1965 *Ariel* and Plath's intended volume. Linda Wagner-Martin notes that using Plath's order, "the book plunged through her most anguished and vituperative poems to end with the emotionally positive bee sequence. . . . With her arrangement, she was telling a story, the story of her life as artist and married woman, and the dissolution of that life" but ending with "a healthy rebirth" (Wagner-Martin, 227). Ronald Hayman observes that "most of the verse invective against Assia [Wevill, Hughes's mistress] is to be found among" the poems

Hughes "held back" (Hayman, 202). Katha Pollitt wonders, "Would it have made a difference to her reputation . . . if Plath's pattern had been preserved, with the last poems added as a separate section? Or even if a complete edition of her poems had appeared, say, ten years ago [1975], when interest in Plath was still high? Well, better late than never."[16]

## New Directions

Pollitt's query suggests the direction Plath studies have taken since the 1981 appearance of *The Collected Poems* and the new, crucial evidence about *Ariel*. As Perloff comments in her 1986 essay, "Only now, more than twenty years after [Plath's] death, can we begin to assess her oeuvre."[17] But even today, her oeuvre may be incomplete. Plath's executors divulged vital information 16 years ago, and one wonders whether further surprises may remain: portions of the Smith collection of Plath manuscripts are sealed until the year 2013, and many questions raised by biographers remain unanswered. Plath scholars of the past three decades have produced excellent work with the materials available to them, but if the historical character of Plath research can be said to predict future efforts, the direction of Plath scholarship promises to be both unpredictable and exciting.

Obviously, the search should continue for primary texts. Are there letters, journals, poems, stories, even a novel in the hands of people whom Plath's estate does not control? The biographers seem to have done a thorough job of finding whatever materials are available, but is there anything else out there to be found, anyone else to be cajoled? Will the death of principal (or even secondary) players in this drama (Plath's and Hughes's families, friends, acquaintances) produce new information? Publication of Plath's *Journals* and *Collected Poems* seems to have raised as many questions as these new volumes have answered: Where are the missing journals and manuscripts? Were they really destroyed? Of what other tinkering may Plath's estate and/or family be guilty?

Plath's suicide has informed and influenced studies of her work and will probably continue to do so. But one line of inquiry motivated by the new *Ariel* information is to focus not on Plath's pathology but on the ways she transformed her healthy and justified anger into art. To regard Plath as Ariel is to provide both motivation and tools for examination. Ariel in her mundane existence is troubled; the only life possible for her is one that casts her in the impossible role of servant and victim.

Like Jerusalem, she is besieged; the storm and tempest and devouring fire that distress that city afflict her as well. She is a Jew, victim of grim atrocities. She is a spouse, both choosing and railing against servitude. She is a wife, wounded by betrayal. She is a woman, victim of a sexual passion that can realize neither viable release nor proper partner. She is a mother, servant to a solitary and fearful parenthood.

Like Jerusalem as well, her expectations are supramundane. Death signals the end of her distress and promises a new existence in which the enemies of Ariel will be punished. But it is also a cataclysmic occurrence whose outcome denies earthly certification. Therefore death is a goal at once intensely desired and greatly feared. At the same time ecstatic and agonized, Ariel gallops, flies, or speeds unflinchingly toward it.

Death is an annealing, transfiguring experience. From it the woman may rise, shedding "dead hands, dead stringencies," to an ecstatic, totally pure union with the Spirit. Ambivalence is resolved in the choice of this marriage partner; he is both Christ the son and God the father, apocalyptic analogues of the choices she has made, but cannot decide between, in earthly life. In death, too, the baby is assured the same eventual triumph. And from death the phoenix may rise to live again.

Essentially Christian in its outlines, this apocalyptic vision belongs wholly to the poet. Plath's poetry is not religious in any strict, literal sense; it is not a vehicle to redisclose the vision of Isaiah and Saint John. Plath's use of biblical materials, like her use of mythical and biographical ones, is metaphorical, a means by which she creates and expresses her individual, compelling vision. The self who emerges from these poems has the energy, strength, and womanly instincts of a lioness, and the death-defying perspective of one who is God's. The poems are not prophetic but apocalyptic; as Plath herself tells us, "I am not gifted with the tongue of Jeremiah, though I may be sleepless enough before my vision of the apocalypse."[18]

# Notes and References

*Chapter One*

1. Sylvia Plath, *Letters Home,* ed. Aurelia Schober Plath (New York: Harper & Row, 1975), 346; hereafter cited in text as *L.*
2. Nancy Hunter Steiner, *A Closer Look at Ariel: A Memory of Sylvia Plath* (New York: Popular Library, 1973), 57.
3. Sylvia Plath, *The Bell Jar* (New York: Harper & Row, 1971), 275; hereafter cited in text as *B.*
4. A. Alvarez, *The Savage God* (New York: Random House, 1971), 6.

*Chapter Two*

1. Janet Malcolm, *The Silent Woman: Sylvia Plath and Ted Hughes* (New York: Alfred A. Knopf, 1994), 154; hereafter cited in text.
2. Edward Butscher, *Sylvia Plath: Method and Madness* (New York: Seabury Press, 1976), 67; hereafter cited in text.
3. Linda W. Wagner-Martin, *Sylvia Plath: A Biography* (New York: Simon & Schuster, 1987), 16; hereafter cited in text.
4. Anne Stevenson, *Bitter Fame: A Life of Sylvia Plath* (Boston: Houghton Mifflin, 1989), xi; hereafter cited in text.
5. Paul Alexander, *Rough Magic: A Biography of Sylvia Plath* (New York: Viking Penguin, 1991), 2; hereafter cited in text.
6. Ronald Hayman, *The Death and Life of Sylvia Plath* (New York: Carol Publishing Group, 1991), xii, xiii; hereafter cited in text.
7. Jacqueline Rose, *The Haunting of Sylvia Plath* (Cambridge: Harvard University Press, 1994), ix; hereafter cited in text.

*Chapter Three*

1. Sylvia Plath, *The Journals of Sylvia Plath,* ed. Ted Hughes and Frances McCullough (New York: The Dial Press, 1982); hereafter cited in text as *J.*
2. Ted Hughes, "Sylvia Plath and Her Journals," in *Ariel Ascending,* ed. by Paul Alexander (New York: Harper & Row, 1985), 152.
3. Edwin McDowell, *New York Times Book Review,* November 14, 1982, 26.
4. Alexander, *Ariel Ascending,* 152n.
5. Hughes, "Sylvia Plath and Her Journals," 152–53.

*Chapter Four*

1. *Johnny Panic and the Bible of Dreams* (New York: Harper & Row, 1979); hereafter cited in text as *JP*.
2. Emily Leider, "Sylvia Plath and Superman," *San Francisco Review of Books* 5 ( June 1979): 24.
3. Margaret Atwood, "Poet's Prose," *New York Times Book Review,* January 28, 1979, 10.
4. Suzanne Juhasz, review of *Johnny Panic and the Bible of Dreams, Library Journal* 103 (December 15, 1978): 2522.
5. Katha Pollitt, "Aesthetic Suicide," *Harper's Magazine* 258 (February 1978): 85.

*Chapter Five*

1. Ted Hughes, "The Chronological Order of Sylvia Plath's Poems," in *The Art of Sylvia Plath,* ed. Charles Newman (Bloomington: Indiana University Press, 1970), 187.
2. Sylvia Plath, *The Collected Poems,* ed. Ted Hughes (New York: Harper & Row, 1981); hereafter cited in text as *CP*.
3. Sylvia Plath, "Temper of Time," *The Nation* 181 (August 6, 1955): 119.
4. Sylvia Plath, "Departure," in *The Colossus* (New York: Alfred A. Knopf, 1962), 18.
5. Sylvia Plath "Lament," *New Orleans Poetry Journal* 1 (October 1955): 19.
6. Sylvia Plath, "Wreath for a Bridal," *Poetry* 89 ( January 1957): 231.
7. Sylvia Plath, "The Other Two," in *Lyonnesse* (London: Rainbow Press, 1971), 26.
8. Sylvia Plath, "Crystal Gazer," in *Crystal Gazer* (London: Rainbow Press, 1971), 17–18.
9. Sylvia Plath, "Admonitions," *Smith Review* (Spring 1954); 23.
10. Sylvia Plath, "Metamorphoses of the Moon," in *Lyonnesse,* 8–9.
11. Sylvia Plath, "Black Rook in Rainy Weather," in *Crossing the Water* (New York: Harper & Row, 1971), 41.
12. M. L. Rosenthal, "Sylvia Plath and Confessional Poetry," in *The Art of Sylvia Plath,* 71.
13. Sylvia Plath, "To Eva Descending the Stair," *Harper's Magazine* 209 (September 1954): 63.
14. Sylvia Plath, "Doomsday," *Harper's Magazine* 208 (May 1954): 29.
15. Sylvia Plath, "The Dream of the Hearse-Driver," in *Crystal Gazer,* 10.
16. Sylvia Plath, "Ocean 1212-W," *The Listener* 70 (August 29, 1963): 313.
17. Sylvia Plath, "Circus in Three Rings," *Atlantic Monthly* 196 (August 1955): 68.
18. Sylvia Plath, "A Winter's Tale," *New Yorker* 35 (December 12, 1959): 116.

19. Sylvia Plath, " 'Some God Got Hold of Me,' " *Village Voice* 16 (October 28, 1971): 30.

20. Sylvia Plath, "Metaphors," in *Crossing the Water,* 43.

21. Sylvia Plath, "Tinker Jack and the Tidy Wives," *Accent* 17 (Autumn 1957): 248.

22. Sylvia Plath, "Ocean 1212-W," 313.

23. Sylvia Plath, "Electra on Azalea Path," *Hudson Review* 13 (Fall 1960): 414–15.

24. Syliva Plath, "Sunday at the Mintons'," *Mademoiselle* 35 (August 1952): 377, 255.

25. Sylvia Plath, "Maenad," in *Crossing the Water,* 51.

26. Aurelia S. Plath, "Letter Written in the Actuality of Spring," in *Ariel Ascending,* 214–16.

27. Charles Newman, "Candor Is the Only Wile—The Art of Sylvia Plath," in *The Art of Sylvia Plath,* 23.

28. Hughes, "The Chronological Order," 192.

*Chapter Six*

1. John Frederick Nims, "The Poetry of Sylvia Plath—A Technical Analysis," in *The Art of Sylvia Plath,* 140–52.

2. Nims, 147–48, 151–52.

3. Douglas Cleverdon, "On *Three Women*," in *The Art of Sylvia Plath,* 227–29.

4. A. Alvarez, "Sylvia Plath," in *The Art of Sylvia Plath,* 60.

5. Sylvia Plath, "Sylvia Plath," interview by Peter Orr, in *The Poet Speaks,* ed. Peter Orr (London: Routledge & Kegan Paul, 1966), 170; hereafter cited in text as *TPS*.

6. Sylvia Plath, "Mayflower," in *Lyonnesse,* 3.

7. Sylvia Plath, *Wreath for a Bridal* (Frensham: The Sceptre Press, 1970), unpaged.

8. Sylvia Plath, "The Goring," in *Crystal Gazer,* 14.

9. Nims, 140.

10. Sylvia Plath, "Snakecharmer," "The Hermit at Outermost House," in *The Colossus,* 9, 54.

11. Sylvia Plath, "Insomniac," *Crossing the Water,* 10–11.

12. Sylvia Plath, "Event" in *Winter Trees,* (New York: Harper & Row, 1972), 16.

13. Richard Wilbur, "The Genie in the Bottle," in *Mid Century American Poets,* ed. John Ciardi (New York: Twayne Publishers, 1950), 7.

14. Helen Vendler, "Crossing the Water,"*New York Times Book Review,* October 10, 1971, 4, 48.

15. Sylvia Plath, "The Tour," in *Winter Trees,* 37–39.

16. Stephen Spender, "Warnings from the Grave," *New Republic* 154 (June 18, 1966): 23; hereafter cited in text.

17. Sylvia Plath, "Kindness," in *Ariel* (New York: Harper & Row, 1966), 82.

*Chapter Seven*

1. Hughes, "The Chronological Order," 192.
2. Ted Hughes, "Note," in *Winter Trees,* front matter.
3. Hughes, "Note," front matter.
4. Sylvia Plath, "Getting There," in *Ariel,* 36–38.
5. A. R. Jones, "Necessity and Freedom: The Poetry of Robert Lowell, Sylvia Plath, and Anne Sexton," *Critical Quarterly* 7 (Spring 1965), 22.
6. Plath, "Ocean 1212-W," 313.
7. Sylvia Plath, "Gigolo," in *Winter Trees,* 2–7
8. Plath, "Ocean 1212-W," 312.
9. Sylvia Plath, "Amnesiac," in *Winter Trees,* 19.
10. Sylvia Plath, "Mystic," in *Winter Trees,* 4–5.
11. Alvarez, "Sylvia Plath," 66.
12. A. R. Jones, "On 'Daddy,' " in *The Art of Sylvia Plath,* 235–36.
13. Cleverdon, 229.
14. Sylvia Plath, "Context," *London Magazine,* February 1962, 46.
15. Robert Lowell, foreword to *Ariel,* ix.
16. Anne Sexton, "The Barfly Ought to Sing," in *The Art of Sylvia Plath,* 175.
17. Sylvia Plath, "Context," 46.

*Chapter Eight*

1. Sylvia Plath, "Ariel," in *Ariel,* 26.
2. Alvarez, "Sylvia Plath," 61.
3. Hughes, "The Chronological Order," 194.
4. William Shakespeare, *The Tempest,* 1.2.242–46, 495–97.
5. Sylvia Plath, "The Hanging Man," in *Ariel,* 69.
6. Sylvia Plath, "Three Women: A Poem for Three Voices," in *Winter Trees,* 50.
7. Sylvia Plath, "Purdah," in *Winter Trees,* 42.
8. Sylvia Plath, "Years," in *Ariel,* 72.
9. Plath, "Three Women: A Poem for Three Voices," 48.
10. Sylvia Plath, "Lady Lazarus," in *Ariel,* 9.
11. Sylvia Plath, "Stings," in *Ariel,* 63.
12. Sylvia Plath, "Fever 103°," in *Ariel,* 54–55.
13. Sylvia Plath, "A Birthday Present," in *Ariel,* 42, 44.
14. Sylvia Plath, "Childless Woman," in *Winter Trees,* 34.
15. Sylvia Plath, "Nick and the Candlestick," in *Ariel,* 34.

16. Sylvia Plath, "Little Fugue," in *Ariel*, 71.
17. Sylvia Plath, "Berck-Plage," in *Ariel*, 22, 25.
18. Robert Scholes, "The Bell Jar," *New York Times Book Review*, April 11, 1971, 7.

*Chapter Nine*

1. Rosenthal, 69.
2. Linda W. Wagner, introduction to *Critical Essays on Sylvia Plath*, ed. Linda W. Wagner (Boston: G. K. Hall, 1984), 2.
3. Helen Vendler, "An Intractable Metal," in *Ariel Ascending*, 5, 8.
4. Laurence Lerner, "Sylvia Plath," in *Critical Essays on Sylvia Plath*, 66.
5. Stanley Plumly, "What Ceremony of Words," in *Ariel Ascending*, 16, 25.
6. Rosenthal, 74.
7. Annette Kolodny, "Dancing through the Minefield: Some Observations on the Theory, Practice, and Politics of a Feminist Literary Criticism," in *The New Feminist Criticism*, ed. Elaine Showalter (New York: Pantheon Books, 1985), 144.
8. Pamela J. Annas, "The Self in the World: The Social Context of Sylvia Plath's Late Poems," in *Critical Essays on Sylvia Plath*, 131.
9. Alicia Ostriker, *Writing Like a Woman* (Ann Arbor: University of Michigan Press, 1983), 45.
10. Susan R. Van Dyne, "More Terrible Than She Ever Was," in *Critical Essays on Sylvia Plath*, 169.
11. Mary Lynn Broe, " 'Enigmatical, Shifting My Clarities,' " in *Ariel Ascending*, 84, 86.
12. Hughes, "The Chronological Order," 193.
13. Hughes, "Note," front matter.
14. Marjorie Perloff, "Sylvia Plath's *Collected Poems:* A Review-Essay," in *Resources for American Literary Study* 11 (Autumn 1981): 305.
15. Marjorie Perloff, "The Two *Ariels*: The (Re)Making of the Sylvia Plath Canon," in *Poems in Their Place*, ed. Neil Fraistat (Chapel Hill: University of North Carolina Press, 1986), 311, 314, 330.
16. Katha Pollitt, "A Note of Triumph," in *Critical Essays on Sylvia Plath*, 68.
17. Perloff, "The Two *Ariels*," 331.
18. Plath, "Context," 46.

# Selected Bibliography

## PRIMARY SOURCES

*Poetry*

*The Colossus and Other Poems.* London: William Heinemann, 1960; New York: Alfred A. Knopf, 1962; London: Faber and Faber, 1976.

*A Winter Ship.* Edinburgh: Tragara Press, 1960.

*Ariel.* London: Faber and Faber, 1965; New York: Harper & Row, 1966.

*Uncollected Poems.* London: Turret Books, 1965. Limited edition of 150 copies.

*Three Women, A Monologue for Three Voices.* London: Turret Books, 1968. Limited edition of 180 copies. Subsequently included in *Winter Trees.*

*Wreath for a Bridal.* Frensham: The Sceptre Press, 1970. Limited edition of 100 copies.

*Crossing the Water.* London: Faber and Faber, 1971; New York: Harper & Row, 1971.

*Crystal Gazer.* London: Rainbow Press, 1971. Limited edition of 400 copies.

*Fiesta Melons.* Exeter, England: Rougemont Press, 1971. Limited edition of 150 copies.

*Lyonnesse.* London: Rainbow Press, 1971. Limited edition of 400 copies.

*Winter Trees.* London: Faber and Faber, 1971; New York: Harper & Row, 1972.

*The Bed Book.* London: Faber and Faber, 1976; New York: Harper & Row, 1976.

*Two Poems.* Bedfordshire, England: Sceptre Press, 1980.

*Two Uncollected Poems.* London: Anvil Press Poetry, 1980.

*The Collected Poems* Edited by Ted Hughes. London: Faber and Faber, 1981; New York: Harper & Row, 1981.

*A Day in June.* Ely, England: Embers Handpress, 1981.

*Dialogue over a Ouija Board.* Cambridge: Rainbow Press, 1981.

*The Green Rock.* Ely, England: Embers Handpress, 1982.

*Selected Poems.* London: Faber and Faber, 1985.


*Fiction*

"And Summer Will Not Come Again." *Seventeen* (March 1950).

*The Bell Jar.* London: William Heinemann, 1963 (published under pseudonym Victoria Lucas); London: Faber and Faber, 1966; New York: Harper & Row, 1971; and New York: Bantam Books, 1972 (with author identified).

*Johnny Panic and the Bible of Dreams.* London: Faber and Faber, 1977; New York: Harper & Row, 1979.

*Nonfiction*

*Letters Home.* Edited by Aurelia Schober Plath. New York: Harper & Row, 1975.
*Johnny Panic and the Bible of Dreams.* London: Faber and Faber, 1977; New York: Harper & Row, 1979.
*The Journals of Sylvia Plath.* Edited by Ted Hughes and Frances McCullough. New York: The Dial Press, 1982.

*Articles, Essays, Interviews (not included in Johnny Panic)*

"Mademoiselle's Last Word on College." *Mademoiselle* 37 (August 1953): 235.
"Poets on Campus." *Mademoiselle* 37 (August 1953): 235.
"Sketchbook of a Spanish Summer." *Christian Science Monitor,* November 5, 1956, 13, and November 6, 1956, 17.
"Pair of Queens." Review. *New Statesman* 63 (April 27, 1962): 602–3.
"Oblongs." Review. *New Statesman* 63 (May 18, 1962): 724.
"The Poet Speaks." BBC interview. Argo records. Also published in *The Poet Speaks,* edited by Peter Orr. London: Routledge & Kegan Paul, 1966.
"Eccentricity." *The Listener* 79 (May 9, 1968): 607.

## SECONDARY SOURCES

*Bibliographies*

Homberger, Eric. *A Chronological Checklist of the Periodical Publications of Sylvia Plath.* Exeter, England: F. E. Raddan and Sons, 1970. American Arts Pamphlet Series, published by the American Arts Documentation Centre at the University of Exeter. Checklist of all poems, short stories, and non-fiction by Sylvia Plath published in periodicals between 1950 and 1969.
Kinzie, Mary. "An Informal Check List of Criticism." In *The Art of Sylvia Plath,* edited by Charles Newman. Bloomington and London: Indiana University Press, 1970. An annotated list of Plath criticism published between 1969 and 1967.
Meyering, Sheryl L. *Sylvia Plath: A Reference Guide, 1973–1988.* Boston: G. K. Hall, 1990. An annotated listing of primary and secondary sources continuing from the year when Northouse and Walsh's bibliography concludes. Useful here as well is Meyering's introduction, which summarizes the nature and development of Plath publication and criticism from the time of Plath's death until the mid-1980s.
Northouse, Cameron, and Thomas P. Walsh. *Sylvia Plath and Anne Sexton: A Reference Guide.* Boston: G. K. Hall, 1974. A listing of poetry and prose (fiction and nonfiction) by Plath published in periodical and in book form between 1952 and 1973, followed by a selected, annotated listing of books and articles about Plath published between 1960 and 1973.
Tabor, Stephen. *Sylvia Plath: An Analytical Bibliography.* Westport, Conn.: Meckler, 1987.

————. *Sylvia Plath: An Annotated Bibliography*. New York, Greenwood Press, 1987.

*Biographies*

Please see chapter 2 for reviews of these biographies.

Alexander, Paul. *Rough Magic: A Biography of Sylvia Plath*. New York: Viking Penguin, 1991. Portrays Plath as a clinically depressed victim of her past and of her husband and sees Hughes as the primary villain of Plath's story.

Butscher, Edward. *Sylvia Plath: Method and Madness*. New York: Seabury Press, 1976. Dismisses Plath as a "bitch goddess."

Hayman, Ronald. *The Death and Life of Sylvia Plath*. New York: Carol Publishing Group, 1991. Attributes Plath's suicide to "the triple convergence of the deep-seated death drive, the demoralizing circumstances in which she was living, and the effects of the [antidepressive] drugs" and argues that "in so far as her suicide was an act of aggression, it was aimed against [her husband, Ted Hughes] and his new lover, Assia Wevill."

Malcolm, Janet. *The Silent Woman: Sylvia Plath & Ted Hughes*. New York: Alfred A. Knopf, 1994. Analyzes the requirements and impulses of biography in general and of Plath's case specifically.

Rose, Jacqueline. *The Haunting of Sylvia Plath*. Cambridge: Harvard University Press, 1991. Evaluates Plath's revelation of herself in her texts.

Stevenson, Anne. *Bitter Fame: A Life of Sylvia Plath*. Boston: Houghton Mifflin, 1989. Aims to correct Wagner-Martin's view by attributing full blame to Plath herself, stressing Plath's "huge mood swings," her "manic violence," and her "paranoia."

Wagner-Martin, Linda W. *Sylvia Plath: A Biography*. New York: Simon & Schuster, 1987. The best of these biographies. Regards Plath as a victim of the extremes of her own personality and, to some degree, of her husband's domination.

*Criticism*

COLLECTIONS

Alexander, Paul. *Ariel Ascending: Writings about Sylvia Plath*. New York: Harper & Row, 1985. The most recent collection of critical essays and personal memoirs. Some of these pieces were previously published, and some are original to this volume. Contents: Paul Alexander, introduction (ix-xv); Helen Vendler, "An Intractable Metal" (1–12); Stanley Plumly, "What Ceremony of Words" (13–25); Joyce Carol Oates, "The Death Throes of Romanticism" (26–45); John Frederick Nims, "The Poetry of Sylvia Plath" (46–60); Barbara Hardy, "Enlargement or Derangement?" (61–79); Mary Lynn Broe, "Enigmatical, Shifting My Clarities" (80–93);

Katha Pollitt, "A Note of Triumph" (94–99); Elizabeth Hardwick, "On Sylvia Plath" (100–115); Rosellen Brown, "Keeping the Self at Bay" (116–124); Howard Moss, "Dying: An Introduction" (125–29); Robert Scholes, "Esther Came Back like a Retreaded Tire" (130–33); Vance Bourjaily, "Victoria Lucas and Elly Higginbottom" (134–51); Ted Hughes, "Sylvia Plath and Her Journals" (152–64); Grace Schulman, "Sylvia Plath and Yaddo" (165–77); Anne Sexton, "The Barfly Ought to Sing" (178–184); A. Alvarez, "Sylvia Plath: A Memoir" (185–213); Aurelia S. Plath, "Letter Written in the Actuality of Spring" (214–17).

Butscher, Edward, ed. *Sylvia Plath: The Woman and the Work*. London: Peter Owen, 1979. A collection of memoirs and essays about Plath ("The Woman") and about her poetry and novel ("The Work"), some commissioned for this anthology and some reprinted. The memoirs are of special biographical interest; those by Lameyer, Krook, Kopp, Roche, and Sigmund appear here for the first time. Contents: Edward Butscher, "In Search of Sylvia: An Introduction" (3–29); memoirs: Richard Wilbur, "Cottage Street, 1953" (a poem) (30–31); Gordon Lameyer, "Sylvia at Smith" (32–41); Laurie Levy, "Outside the Bell Jar" (42–48); Dorothea Krook, "Recollections of Sylvia Plath" (49–60); Jane Baltzell Kopp, " 'Gone, Very Gone Youth': Sylvia Plath at Cambridge, 1955–1957" (61–80); Clarissa Roche, "Sylvia Plath: Vignettes from England" (81–96); Paula Rothholz, "For Sylvia at 4:30 A.M." (a poem) (97–99); Elizabeth Sigmund, "Sylvia in Devon: 1962" (101–107) Critical Essays: Pamela Smith, "Architectonics: Sylvia Plath's Colossus" (111–24); Marjorie G. Perloff, "On the Road to *Ariel*: The 'Transitional' Poetry of Sylvia Plath" ( 125–42); Gordon Lameyer, "The Double in Sylvia Plath's *The Bell Jar*" ( 143–65); Constance Scheerer, "The Deathly Paradise of Sylvia Plath" ( 166–76); Arthur K. Oberg, "Sylvia Plath and the New Decadence" (177–85); Robert Phillips, "The Dark Funnel: A Reading of Sylvia Plath" (186–205); Joyce Carol Oates, "The Death Throes of Romanticism: The Poetry of Sylvia Plath" (206–24); Irving Howe, "The Plath Celebration: A Partial Dissent" (225–35).

Newman, Charles, ed. *The Art of Sylvia Plath*. Bloomington and London: Indiana University Press, 1970. The first collection of articles about Sylvia Plath, including critical essays about Plath's poetry and novel, biographical essays, and reviews. The appendix includes a selection of Plath's work, some of Plath's pen drawings, and a bibliography. Many excellent critical essays on Plath, which appeared originally in journals, are reprinted in this book; these are not listed under "Biographies" or "Criticism: Essays and Reviews" in this bibliography. Contents: Charles Newman, "Candor Is the Only Wile—The Art of Sylvia Plath" (21–55); A. Alvarez, "Sylvia Plath" (56–68); M. L. Rosenthal, "Sylvia Plath and Confessional Poetry" (69–76); Richard Howard, "Sylvia Plath: 'And I

Have No Face, I Have Wanted to Efface Myself . . .' " (77–88); Edward
Lucie-Smith, "Sea-imagery in the Work of Sylvia Plath" (91–99);
Annette Lavers, "The World as Icon—On Sylvia Plath's Themes"
(100–135); John Frederick Nims, "The Poetry of Sylvia Plath—A Tech-
nical Analysis" (136–52); Lois Ames, "Notes toward a Biography"
(155–73); Anne Sexton, "The Barfly Ought to Sing" (174–81); Wendy
Campbell, "Remembering Sylvia" (182–86); Ted Hughes, "The Chronological Order of Sylvia Plath's Poems" (187–95); Stephen Spender,
"Warnings from the Grave" (199–203); A. E. Dyson, "On Sylvia Plath"
(204–10); George Steiner, "Dying Is an Art" (211–18); Mary Ellmann,
"*The Bell Jar*—An American Girlhood" (221–26); Douglas Cleverdon,
"On *Three Women*" ( 227–29); A. R. Jones, "On 'Daddy' " (230–36);
appendix.

Wagner, Linda W., ed. *Critical Essays on Sylvia Plath*. Boston: G. K. Hall, 1984.
A collection of reviews and essays on Plath's poetry and fiction, some
reprinted and some original in this volume. Wagner's useful and insightful introductory essay (1–24) discusses critical approaches to and evalua-
tions of Plath's work by the reviewers and essayists of this collection,
assessing their treatment of prominent theories about and themes within
Plaths's poetry, fiction, and nonfiction prose. Contents: reviews of *The
Colossus* by A. E. Dyson (27–30), E. Lucas Myers (30–32), M. L. Rosenthal (32–34); of *The Bell Jar* by Mason Harris (34–38); of *Ariel* by Peter
Davison (38–41), Barbara Drake (42–43), Robert L. Stilwell (44–45);
of *Crossing the Water* by Peter Porter (46–47), Paul West ( 48–51), Douglas Dunn (51–53); of *Winter Trees* by Damian Grant (53–55), Alan
Brownstone (55–56); of *Letters Home* by Jo Brans (56–59), Carol Bere
(59–62); of *Johnny Panic and the Bible of Dreams* by Douglas Hill
(62–64); of *The Collected Poems* by Laurence Lerner (64–67), Katha Pollitt (67–72), William H. Pritchard (72–77); of *The Journals of Sylvia Plath*
by Nancy Milford (77–83). Essays: Leonard Sanazaro, "The Transfiguring Self: Sylvia Plath, A Reconsideration" (87–97); Alicia Ostriker, "The
Americanization of Sylvia" (97–109); Marjorie Perloff, "*Angst* and Animism in the Poetry of Sylvia Plath" (109–24); Guinevara A. Nance and
Judith P. Jones, "Doing Away with Daddy: Exorcism and Sympathetic
Magic in Plath's Poetry" (124–30); Pamela J. Annas, "The Self in the
World: The Social Context of Sylvia Plath's Late Poems" (130–39); Fred-
erick Buell, "Sylvia Plath's Traditionalism" (140–54); Susan R. Van
Dyne, " 'More Terrible Than She Ever Was': The Manuscripts of Sylvia
Plath's Bee Poems" (154–70); Margaret Dickie, "Sylvia Plath's Narra-
tive Strategies" (170–82); Melody Zajdel, "Apprenticed in a Bible of
Dreams: Sylvia Plath's Short Stories" (182–93); Roberta Mazzanti,
"Plath in Italy" (193–204); Sandra M. Gilbert, "In Yeats' House: The
Death and Resurrection of Sylvia Plath" (204–22).

BOOKS

Aird, Eileen. *Sylvia Plath: Her Life and Work*. New York: Harper & Row, 1973. A general study of Plath's writing. For easy reference, separate chapters provide a short biography (chap. 1), studies of each of Plath's commercially published volumes of poetry (chaps. 2–5), an analysis of *The Bell Jar* (chap. 6), and a general examination of the "interrelated symbols and image clusters" Plath uses most frequently (chap. 7).

Alvarez, A. *The Savage God*. New York: Random House, 1971. A study of suicide and the artist's special vulnerability to it. Part 1 focuses on Sylvia Plath specifically; the rest of the book mentions her here and there.

Annas, Pamela J. *A Disturbance in Mirrors: The Poetry of Sylvia Plath*. New York: Greenwood Press, 1988.

Axelrod, Stephen G. *Sylvia Plath: The Wound and the Cure of Words*. Baltimore: Johns Hopkins University Press, 1991. A study, combining psychoanalytic and literary critical approaches, of Plath's "struggle for voice."

Bassnet, Susan. *Sylvia Plath*. New York: Barnes and Noble Books, 1987. Women Writers Series. An analysis that approaches Plath's poetry by means of topical and biographical subjects.

Broe, Mary L. *Protean Poetic: The Poetry of Sylvia Plath*. Columbia: University of Missouri Press, 1980. A chronologically arranged analysis of Plath's poetry.

Holbrook, David. *Sylvia Plath: Poetry and Existence*. Atlantic Highlands, New Jersey: Humanities Press, 1976. A valuable psychological study of Plath both as an individual and as a contemporary artist as a means of providing insight into her poetry.

Kroll, Judith. *Chapters in a Mythology: The Poetry of Sylvia Plath*. New York: Harper & Row, 1976. A study of the "thematic meaning of Plath's late poems." This book is especially useful for its discussion of Plath's imagery, for its exploration of her mythic and literary sources, and for its close reading of several specific poems.

Marsack, Robyn. *Sylvia Plath*. Buckingham, Great Britain: Open University Press, 1992. Open Guides to Literature Series. A study of Plath's poetry intended to be used in conjunction with *The Collected Poems*. The book is arranged for teaching by first asking questions and then discussing possible answers.

Melander, Ingrid. *The Poetry of Sylvia Plath: A Study of Themes*. Stockholm: Almquist & Wiksell, 1972. Gothenburg Studies in English 25. Thematic analysis of Plath's poetry. Three basic themes are examined: the relationship between father and daughter, the sense of estrangement from or hostility in nature, and death.

Steiner, Nancy Hunter. *A Closer Look at Ariel: A Memory of Sylvia Plath*. New York: Popular Library, 1973. An insightful and valuable memoir of Plath's college years by her college roommate, with an excellent introduction by George Stade.

ESSAYS AND REVIEWS

Alvarez, A. "The Prison of Prose." Review of *Johnny Panic and the Bible of Dreams. Observer,* October 16, 1977, 36.

Atwood, Margaret. "Poet's Prose." Review of *Johnny Panic. New York Times Book Review,* January 28, 1979, 10.

Bradley, Debra. "Smith Acquires Papers of Poet Sylvia Plath." *Daily Hampshire Gazette,* September 17, 1981, 1. (Smith's purchase, parts of which are sealed for 50 yrs . . .)

Broe, Mary Lynn. " 'Oh Dad, Poor Dad': Sylvia Plath's Comic Exorcism." *Notes on Contemporary Literature* 9 (January 1979): 2–4. Humor in "Daddy."

Claire, William F. "That Rare, Random Descent: The Poetry and Pathos of Sylvia Plath." *Antioch Review* 26 (Winter 1966): 552–60. An exploration of Plath's uniquely modern and confessional qualities.

Cooley, Peter. "Autism, Autoeroticism, Auto-da-fe: The Tragic Poetry of Sylvia Plath." *Hollins Critic* 10 (February 1973): 1–15. A review by an important contemporary poet of Plath's early, transitional, and late poems, with special attention given to the persona in *Ariel.*

Cox, C. B., and A. R. Jones. "After the Tranquillized Fifties: Notes on Sylvia Plath and James Baldwin." *Critical Quarterly* 6 (Summer 1964): 107–22. An important essay in Plath criticism, marking a very early, wholly serious approach to her as an artist. A portion was later reprinted as "On Daddy," by Jones, in *The Art of Sylvia Plath.*

Davison, Peter. " 'Inhabited by a Cry': The Last Poetry of Sylvia Plath." *Atlantic Monthly* 218 (August 1966): 76–77. A brief but useful *Ariel* review. With these late poems as evidence, Davison praises the maturity of Plath's art, noting that her work's highly emotional quality should not obscure that "a true poet" wrote it. Her poems "are a triumph for poetry, in fact, at the moment that they are a defeat for their author."

Donovan, Josephine. "Sexual Politics in Sylvia Plath's Short Stories." *Minnesota Review* 4 (Spring 1973): 150–57. An examination of five stories ("The Wishing Box," "The Fifteen-Dollar Eagle," "The Daughters of Blossom Street," "The Fifty-ninth Bear," and "Johnny Panic and the Bible of Dreams") that illustrate dominance and suppression in male-female psychological and political conflict.

Ehrenpreis, Irvin. "The Other Sylvia Plath." Review of *The Collected Poems. New York Review of Books* 29 (February 4, 1982): 22–24.

Gilbert, Sandra. " 'My Name Is Darkness': The Poetry of Self-Definition." *Contemporary Literature* 19 (Autumn 1976): 443–57.

———. " 'A Fine, White Flying Myth': Confessions of a Plath Addict." *Massachusetts Review* 19 (Autumn 1978): 585–603. " 'A Fine, White Flying Myth': The Life/Work Sylvia Plath." In *Shakespeare's Sisters.* Edited by Sandra M. Gilbert and Susan Gubar. Bloomington: Indiana University Press, 1979, 245–60.

Hardwick, Elizabeth. "On Sylvia Plath." *New York Review of Books* 17 (August 12, 1971): 3–6. Review of *The Bell Jar* and *Crossing the Water* that examines Plath's predominant attitudes and themes, paying special attention to her fascination with death.

Hill, Douglas. "Living and Dying." Review of *Johnny Panic*. *Canadian Forum* 58 (June–July 1978): 32–33.

Himelick, Raymond. "Notes on the Care and Feeding of Nightmares: Burton, Erasmus, and Sylvia Plath." *Western Humanities Review* 28 (Autumn 1974): 313–26. A study of the ways in which *The Bell Jar,* although generically similar to Burton's *Anatomy of Melancholy* and Erasmus's *In Praise of Folly,* projects a uniquely twentieth-century sensibility.

Holbrook, David. "R. D. Laing and the Death Circuit." *Encounter* 31 (August 1968): 34–45. A psychoanalytic approach concerned with theories of sanity and suicide; examines Plath's emphasis on death as a means of rebirth.

Howe, Irving. "Sylvia Plath: A Partial Disagreement." *Harper's Magazine* (January 1972), 88–91. A provocative essay suggesting that Plath's work does not merit the critical acclaim it had recently received.

Hughes, Olwyn. "Letter to the Editor." *New York Review of Books* (September 30, 1976): 42–43. This letter takes a negative view of Edward Butscher's biography (*Sylvia Plath: Method and Madness,* 1975), asserting that it is "rubbishy" and not "worthy of . . . attention."

Jones, A. R. "Necessity and Freedom: The Poetry of Robert Lowell, Sylvia Plath, and Anne Sexton." *Critical Quarterly* 7 (Spring 1965:), 11–30. Of major significance in this essay is Jones's use and definition of the term "confessional" and his early consideration of a "confessional" movement in modern American poetry.

Juhasz, Suzanne. Review of *Johnny Panic and the Bible of Dreams*. *Library Journal* 103 (December 15, 1978): 2522.

Kenner, Hugh. "Sweet Seventeen." Review of *Letters Home*. *National Review* 18 (April 30, 1976): 459–60.

Kinzie, Mary. "A New Life and Other Plath Controversies." *American Poetry Review* 5 (March–April 1976): 5–8. Review of *Letters Home* that compares Edward Butscher's Plath (in *Sylvia Plath: Method and Madness*) with the Plath in *Letters Home*.

Leider, Emily. "Sylvia Plath and Superman." Review of *Johnny Panic*. *San Francisco Review of Books* 5 (June 1979): 23–24.

Libby, Anthony. "God's Lioness and the Priest of Sycorax: Plath and Hughes." *Contemporary Literature* 15 (Summer 1974): 386–405. An exploration of Plath's and Hughes's psychological influence on each other as revealed in their similar poetic concerns, as a way of defining the individual vision of each.

Maloff, Saul. "The Poet as Cult Goddess." *Commonweal* 103 (June 4, 1976): 371–74. A provocative bit of negative criticism. Maloff contends that the proliferating critical-biographical works on Plath create a myth that inflates the ordinary, but has little factual validity.

McDowell, Edwin. "Time Capsule: 2013." *New York Times Book Review,* November 14, 1982, 34. Concerns the new Sylvia Plath Collection at Smith College, rare book room.

Oates, Joyce Carol. "The Death Throes of Romanticism: The Poems of Sylvia Plath." *Southern Review,* n.s. 9 (Summer 1973): 501–22. An excellent and perceptive essay in which Oates, assuming Plath's significance as an artist and "as a cultural phenomenon," explores and defines both the individual and the cultural meaning of Plath's attitudes and dilemmas, as realized in her writing.

Perloff, Marjorie G. "*Angst* and Animism in the Poetry of Sylvia Plath." *Journal of Modern Literature* 1 (1970): 57–74. An intelligent and well-documented essay, one of several published in 1970 to indicate growing critical attention to Plath as a major literary artist (also published in 1970: *The Art of Sylvia Plath*). Perloff explores Plath's poetry, especially the late work, in light of its paradoxical concern with animate and inanimate materials.

———. "Icon of the Fifties." Parnassus 12 and 13: 282–85. An informative description of Plath's embodiment of "the dominant ideology of the Fifties and early Sixties."

———. "On the Road to Ariel: The 'Transitional' Poetry of Sylvia Plath." *Iowa Review* 4 (Spring 1973): 94–110. An examination of ways in which Plath's so-called transitional poems are thematically similar but structurally inferior to the late poems. Perloff suggests that the perspective afforded by publication of the transitional volume diminishes the impressiveness of *Ariel.*

———. "Sylvia Plath's *The Collected Poems.*" Review of *The Collected Poems. Resources for American Literary Study* 11 (Autumn 1981): 304–13.

———. "The Two Ariels: The (Re)Making of the Sylvia Plath Canon." In *Poems in Their Place.* Edited by Neil Fraistat. Chapel Hill: University of North Carolina Press, 1986, 308–33. (The *Ariel* Plath intended would have made a very different impression than the one actually published by Hughes . . .)

Phillips, Robert. "The Dark Funnel: A Reading of Sylvia Plath," *Modern Poetry Studies* 3 (Autumn 1972): 49–74. Phillips explores his theory that the imagery of destruction in Plath's poems and novel results from the poet's reaction to her father's death, which Phillips calls the "central myth" of her imagination.

Pollitt, Katha. "Aesthetic Suicide." Review of *Johnny Panic. Harper's Magazine* 258 (February 1979): 83–86.

Rosenstein, Harriet. "Reconsidering Sylvia Plath." *Ms.* (September 1972): 44–51, 96–99. Asserting that Plath has been "falsely assigned" her "role as feminist heroine," Rosenstein examines the attitudes and temperaments of Plath's women.

Scholes, Robert. *"The Bell Jar."* *New York Times Book Review,* April 11, 1971, 7. An excellent review of *The Bell Jar* on the occasion of its first American publication is astute, thought-provoking, and most enjoyable to read.

Schreiber, Le Anne. Review of *The Journals of Sylvia Plath. New York Times,* April 21, 1982, C-21.

Smith, Stan. "Attitudes Counterfeiting Life: The Irony of Artifice in Sylvia Plath's *The Bell Jar.*" *Critical Quarterly* 17 (Autumn 1975): 247–60. An elaboration of Smith's view that *The Bell Jar,* not merely a psychological case history, is a "highly and originally structured novel."

Thompson, Jan. Review of *Johnny Panic and the Bible of Dreams. Ambit* 73 (1978): 88–89.

Thwaite, Anthony. " 'I Have Never Been So Happy in My Life': On Sylvia Plath." Review of *Letters Home. Encounter* 46 ( June 1976): 64–67.

Vendler, Helen. *"Crossing the Water,"* *New York Times Book Review,* October 10, 1971, 4, 48. This review of *Crossing the Water* is one of the most enlightening of Plath's transitional poems. Vendler analyzes the unique qualities of the work of this period.

Wagner, Linda W. " 'Ariel': 'Auspicious Gales.' " *Concerning Poetry* 10 (Fall 1977): 5–7.

———. "Plath's 'Lady Lazarus.' " *Explicator* 41 (Fall 1982): 50–52.

———. "Sylvia Plath's Specialness in Her Short Stories." *Journal of Narrative Technique* 15 (Winter 1986): 1–14. An analysis of several Plath stories, including some in the Plath Archive at the Lilly Library at Indiana University, to demonstrate the predominance of themes of isolation and individual difference.

# Index

# The Author

Caroline King Barnard Hall earned her B.A., M.A., and Ph.D. (1973) in English at Brown University. She is associate professor of English and women's studies at Pennsylvania State University, Beaver Campus, and is also the author of *Sylvia Plath* (1978) and *Anne Sexton* (1989) in Twayne's United States Authors Series. In addition, she has published articles and papers on Ellen Glasgow, twentieth-century American literature, and women's studies. Hall has held senior Fulbright lectureships in Berlin, Copenhagen, and Klagenfurt, Austria.

# The Editor

Joseph M. Flora earned his B.A. (1956), M.A. (1957), and Ph.D. (1962) in English at the University of Michigan. In 1962 he joined the faculty of the University of North Carolina, where he is professor of English. His study *Hemingway's Nick Adams* (1984) won the Mayflower Award. He is also author of *Vardis Fisher* (1962), *William Ernest Henley* (1970), *Frederick Manfred* (1974), and *Ernest Hemingway: A Study of the Short Fiction* (1989). He is editor of *The English Short Story* (1985) and coeditor of *Southern Writers: A Biographical Dictionary* (1970), *Fifty Southern Writers before 1900* (1987), and *Fifty Southern Writers after 1900* (1987). He serves on the editorial boards of *Studies in Short Fiction* and *Southern Literary Journal*.